P9-DTD-536

PRAISE FOR *THE GOD WHO WEEPS*

"I read this fine book in order better to understand what Mormons believe about divine compassion, and it certainly gave me that. But more important: I received in reading it some deeply personal lessons about the tears of God."

—RICHARD J. MOUW, PH.D., President and Professor of Christian Philosophy, Fuller Theological Seminary

"Writing from the perspective of Mormon faith, Terryl and Fiona Givens have produced a work of theological reflection that has much to offer not only to Latter-day Saints, but to intellectually and morally serious men and women of every religious persuasion who ponder the mystery of a God who, though profoundly transcendent, reveals Himself to us, offers us His friendship, and even shares our joys and sorrows. To be sure, readers who are not Latter-day Saints will learn from *The God Who Weeps* a great deal about what Mormons believe (including certain distinctively Mormon doctrines) and why they believe it. But that is only part of the value of the book. For even readers who do not share certain fundamental tenets of the LDS faith, but who believe in a personal, omnipotent, and omniscient God, will benefit from the Givens' thoughtful reflections on how such a God enters into the lives of imperfect creatures like ourselves, lighting our paths, lifting us up when we fall, and summoning us to share in His divine life."

—ROBERT P. GEORGE, McCormick Professor of Jurisprudence, Princeton University, author of *The Meaning of Marriage: Family, State, Market, and Morals*

"Terryl Givens, one of current Mormonism's most celebrated thinkers, with Fiona Givens here provides a fresh perspective on a number of distinctively LDS teachings. *The God Who Weeps* is a stirring and sensitive look into a personal God whose passions include an infinite capacity to feel after and respond eagerly to the pains and pleadings of His children; a life before this life for both Deity and humanity; a refusal to adopt the classical Christian view of original sin and the dismal and discouraging picture of the human race it paints; and, an optimistic glimpse into a divine plan that seeks to save all of those who wish to be saved. This important work provides a substantive optimism, a welcome and needed portrayal of humanity's heavenly possibilities."

—ROBERT L. MILLET, Professor of Religious Education at Brigham Young University, author of *Grace Works*

"Reading this book is like experiencing Mormonism in high definition. By masterfully weaving together insights from 'the best books'—scripture and literature, theology and philosophy—Terryl and Fiona Givens bring new depth to the fundamentals of their faith. Whether you know a lot or a little about Latter-day Saint doctrine, this book will both educate and inspire you."

—David E. Campbell, Professor of Political Science, University of Notre Dame, Author of *American Grace: How Religion Divides and Unites Us*

"Anyone desiring to understand more about Mormon Christianity could find no better guides than Terryl and Fiona Givens. Their heartfelt testimony to what their faith tradition has taught them about life is enriched with luminous insights from Western literature and philosophy. A lovely book!"

—Mary Ann Glendon, Learned Hand Professor of Law at Harvard and former US Ambassador to the Vatican, author of *The Forum and the Tower: How Scholars and Politicians Have Imagined the World from Plato to Eleanor Roosevelt*

"*The God Who Weeps* is an elegant meditation on the basic tenets of the Mormon faith. The Givenses write with precision and poetry. Their literary and religious references are unusually rich and varied: they include the classic texts of the Bible, early Christian thinkers, Enlightenment philosophers, Romantic poets, German theologians, Russian and American novelists—and many, many more. The prose is at times urgent and even soaring.

"Mormons will enjoy this succinct, sophisticated and searching précis of their core beliefs. Non-Mormons will be led into the heart of a religion that was born on American soil, and whose history is one of the great neglected narratives of our national life."

—Helen Whitney, producer of *The Mormons* and *Faith and Doubt at Ground Zero*

"What if God were everything we are, only perfectly so? And what if those perfections included our vulnerability, our suffering, and our joy? In the Givens' masterful hands, the Mormon view of God comes alive in fresh and challenging ways. Mainstream Christians have much to learn from Mormonism, and this book is the place to start."

—Stephen H. Webb, professor of Religion and Philosophy, Wabash College, author of *Jesus Christ, Eternal God*

"This is not the kind of book Latter-day Saints ordinarily write. It begins at a deep point of human experience where all is uncertain. It asks: how do you move from an elemental condition of ignorance and yearning to belief and faith? The Givenses tell us not only where they end up but how they got there and along the way confront the most baffling moral and intellectual conundrums of human existence."

—Richard Bushman, Gouverneur Morris Professor of History, Emeritus, Columbia University, author of *Joseph Smith, Rough Stone Rolling*

THE GOD WHO WEEPS

THE GOD WHO WEEPS

HOW MORMONISM MAKES SENSE OF LIFE

TERRYL GIVENS
FIONA GIVENS

Library of Congress Cataloging-in-Publication Data

Givens, Terryl, author.
The God who weeps : how Mormonism makes sense of life / Terryl L. Givens ; Fiona Givens.
pages cm
Includes bibliographical references and index.
ISBN 978-1-60907-188-2 (hardbound : alk. paper)
1. Plan of salvation (Mormon theology) 2. Mormon cosmology. 3. God—Attributes. 4. Christian life—Mormon authors. 5. The Church of Jesus Christ of Latter-day Saints—Doctrines. 6. Mormon Church—Doctrines. I. Givens, Fiona, author. II. Title.
BX8643.S25G58 2012
230'.9332—dc23 2012023469

Printed in the United States of America
R. R. Donnelley, Crawfordsville, IN

10 9 8

To Dale and Paula

Who have become acquainted

with the weeping God

Contents

INTRODUCTION

The Longing Soul

"For He satisfyeth the longing soul,
and filleth the hungry soul with goodness."

Whether by design or by chance, we find ourselves in a universe filled with mystery. No picture ever painted fully explains the vast landscape of human experience. Science doesn't try to, and religion often fails. But we humans are meaning-making machines. We are complex creatures of logic and superstition, who crave both clarity and wonder. Faith often asks us to turn a blind eye to the incongruities and inconsistencies of belief in the divine. But reason comes up short as well in accounting for those moments of deepest love and yearning, of unspeakable calm in the midnight of anguish, of the shards of light visible to the inner eye alone.

Skeptics may point out that, even if an all-powerful God presides over creation, we have no guarantee, and little evidence, that such a Being would be any more benevolent and merciful than the frightening figures of a hundred mythologies. Such a concern is reasonable. Most of us do indeed walk our weary way in the dark from candle to candle, or live lives of quiet desperation devoid of even those glimmering guideposts. We are mired in the mundane—and then unexpectedly beauty irrupts into our lives, flashing before us like the first goldfinch of spring. We recognize and crave goodness and kindness, and our hearts yearn to find their source. We know what it is to love beyond any Darwinian drive to preserve our species. We know what it is to mourn the loss of life as something profoundly wrong: too wasteful, too incongruous with the economy of the universe, to be final. We feel to protest the patent absurdity of a one act play:

> To see the golden sun, the azure sky, the outstretched ocean; to walk upon the green earth, and be lord of a thousand creatures; to look down yawning precipices or over distant sunny vales; to see the world spread out under one's feet on a map; to bring the stars near; to view the smallest insects through a microscope; . . . to witness the change of seasons, of spring and autumn, of winter and summer; to feel hot and cold, pleasure and pain, beauty and deformity, right and wrong; to be sensible to the accidents of nature; to consider the mighty world of eye and ear; to listen to the stock-dove's notes amid the forest deep; to journey over moor and mountain; to hear the midnight sainted choir; to visit lighted halls, or the cathedral's gloom, or sit in crowded theatres and see life itself mocked; to study the works of art and refine the sense of beauty to agony; . . . to overlook the world as if time and nature poured their treasures at our feet—to be and to do all this and then in a moment to be nothing! . . .

Whatever sense we make of this world, whatever value we place upon our lives and relationships, whatever meaning we ultimately give to our joys and agonies, must necessarily be a gesture of faith.

Whether we consider the whole a product of impersonal cosmic forces, a malevolent deity, or a benevolent god, depends not on the evidence, but on what we choose, deliberately and consciously, to conclude from that evidence. To our minds, this fork in our mental road is very much the point. It is, in fact, inescapable. James Stephen noted that "in nearly all the important transactions in life, indeed in all transactions whatever which have relation to the future, we have to take a leap in the dark, . . .to act upon very imperfect evidence. . . . I believe it to be the same with religious belief. . . . If we decide to leave the [questions] unanswered, that is a choice; if we waver in our answer that, too, is a choice: but whatever choice we make, we make it at our peril."

It is true that some people seem born with a capacity to readily believe. And many people die with a full complement of faith. A dear relative spent her last months pining for death because she was the last of her generation, she "missed her people" to an excruciating degree, and she grew more and more disconnected from a world she saw as simply irrelevant, without the power to interest or lay hold upon her. It was striking to watch the world and persons beyond the grave assume, in her mind and in her conversation, a fully fleshed-out texture and presence that utterly displaced the inhabitants of the here and now. Faith did not seem a choice for her. It descended upon her as naturally and irresistibly as the heavy snow that fell on her upstate New York farm.

Such a gift we have not found to be common. And it would seem that among those who most vigorously pursue a rational understanding of the universe, who ask the hard questions and follow where they lead, faith is as often a casualty as it is a product. If there is a god, then perhaps as Robert Bolt's Thomas More suggests, "He made the angels to show Him splendor, as He made animals for innocence and plants for their simplicity. But Man He made to serve Him wittily, in the tangle of His mind." Reason must be a part of any solution to the mystery of life that we find satisfactory. A supreme deity would no more gift us with intellect and expect us to forsake it in moments of bafflement, than He would fashion us eyes to see and bid us shut them to the stars. Our vision draws us to that which lies beyond our ken—too distant, or too small, for our mortal powers of perception. Yet we do not abandon our gift of sight, but fashion Galileo's telescope or the electron microscope, which together with naked eyes unlocks new worlds.

So must reason work with will to fashion understanding. The call to faith is a summons to engage the heart, to attune it to resonate in sympathy with principles and values and ideals that we devoutly hope are true *and which we have reasonable but not certain grounds for believing to be true*. There must be grounds for doubt as well as belief, in order to render the choice more truly a choice, and therefore the more deliberate, and laden with personal vulnerability and investment. An overwhelming preponderance of evidence on either side would make our choice as meaningless as would a loaded gun pointed at our heads. The option to believe must appear on one's personal horizon like the fruit of paradise, perched precariously between sets of demands held in dynamic tension.

Fortunately, in this world, one is always provided with sufficient materials out of which to fashion a life of credible conviction or dismissive denial. We are acted upon, in other words, by appeals to our personal values, our yearnings, our fears, our appetites, and our egos. What we choose to embrace, to be responsive to, is the purest reflection of who we are and what we love. That is why faith, the choice to believe, is, in the final analysis, an action that is positively laden with moral significance.

We are, as reflective, thinking, pondering seekers, much like the proverbial ass of Buridan. The beast in the parable starves to death because he is faced with two equally desirable and equally accessible piles of hay. Having no determinative reason to choose one over the other, he perishes in indecision. In the case of us mortals, we are confronted with a world in which there are appealing arguments for a Divinity that is a childish projection, for prophets as scheming or deluded imposters, and for scriptures as so much fabulous fiction. But there is also compelling evidence that a glorious Divinity presides over the cosmos, that His angels are strangers we have entertained unaware, and that His word and will are made manifest through a scriptural canon that is never definitively closed.

There is, as with the ass of Buridan, nothing to compel an individual's preference for one over the other. For most of us, at least, there is neither a choir of heavenly heralds proving God exists, nor a laboratory of science equipment proving He doesn't. Rather, we find a persuasive body of evidence on both sides of life's competing propositions. Only in the case of us mortals, there *is* something to tip the scale. There is something to predispose us to a life of faith or a life of disbelief. There is a heart that, in these conditions of equilibrium and balance, equally "enticed by the one or the other," is truly free to choose belief or skepticism, faith or faithlessness.

The call to faith, in this light, is not some test of a coy god, waiting to see if we "get it right." It is the only summons, issued under the only conditions, which can allow us fully to reveal who we are, what we most love, and what we most devoutly desire. Without constraint, without any form of mental compulsion, the act of belief becomes the freest possible projection of what resides in our hearts. Like the poet's image of a church bell that only reveals its latent music when struck, or a dragonfly that only flames forth its beauty in flight, so does the content of a human heart lie buried until action calls it forth. The greatest act of self-revelation occurs when we *choose* what we will believe, in that space of freedom that exists between knowing that a thing is, and knowing that a thing is not.

This is the realm where faith operates, and when faith is a freely chosen gesture, it expresses something essential about the self. For we do indeed create gods after our own image—or potential image. And that is an activity endowed with incalculable moral meaning. If we linger in indecision, as does Buridan's beast, we will not perish.

We will simply miss an opportunity to act decisively in the absence of certainty, and show that our fear of error is greater than our love of truth.

In what follows, we explore five propositions pertaining to who presides over this universe, where we came from, why we are here, and what might await us in the "undiscovered country." Woven together into a coherent tapestry, we find these concepts compelling, inspiring, and reasonable.

1. *God is a personal entity, having a heart that beats in sympathy with human hearts, feeling our joy and sorrowing over our pain.*

That God has a heart that beats in sympathy with ours is *the* reality that draws us to Him. That He feels real sorrow, rejoices with real gladness, and weeps real tears with us. This, as the prophet Enoch learned, is an awful, terrible, yet infinitely comforting truth.

2. *We lived as spirit beings in the presence of God before we were born into this mortal life.*

A sense of unease in the world and the poignant yearnings and shadowy intimations of an eternal past, attest to a timeless heritage at the core of human identity. As premortal individuals, possessing self-awareness and the power of choice, we existed in God's presence long before the foundations of the earth were laid.

3. *Mortality is an ascent, not a fall, and we carry infinite potential into a world of sin and sorrow.*

Children are born pure and innocent, without the taint of original sin. (We find plenty on our own.) The momentous choice made by Eve and Adam was itself fortunate, insofar as it did not unleash the double specter of depravity and universal condemnation, but rather made possible the introduction of the human family into the schoolhouse of the world.

4. *God has the desire and the power to unite and elevate the entire human family in a kingdom of heaven, and, except for the most stubbornly unwilling, that will be our destiny.*

In the premortal world, God "found Himself in the midst of

spirits and glory," took compassion on these beings, and "saw proper to institute laws whereby the rest . . . could have a privilege to advance like Himself and be exalted with Him." His design was to elevate and ennoble the entire human family. He does not capriciously foreordain any to damnation. And life is not a lottery in which only the fortunate few born at the right time and place receive a winning ticket. God's plan is wise enough, His love generous enough, that none will be left out.

5. *Heaven will consist of those relationships that matter most to us now.*

The same Bible that holds out the promise of joint-heirship with Christ also provides morality tales against excessive ambition. Clearly, to aspire to *be* God is sin; to desire to be *like* God is filial love and devotion. So any concept of eternal life must be framed by the invitation to share in the divine nature. And God's nature and life are the simple extenuation of that which is most elemental, and most worthwhile, about our life here on earth.

CHAPTER ONE

His Heart Is Set upon Us

God is a personal entity,
having a heart that beats in sympathy
with human hearts, feeling our joy and
sorrowing over our pain.

"For He has set his heart upon us."

Is faith the beginning of a quest, or the end? Do "religious people" start out from a posture of belief and interpret the world through that lens, or do they weigh the evidence, and come around to God by way of conclusion? We must recognize at the onset that both militant atheism and fervent theism are the same in this regard: they are both just as likely to serve as a dogmatic point of departure, as they are to be a thoughtful and considered end point in one's journey toward understanding.

In our experience most believers, like doubters, are continually adjusting their paradigms to make better sense of the world as they experience it. Belief is fluid. So is doubt. Disillusion and readjustment work in both directions. Those who come late on the road to Damascus, and see the light at last, remember all those times they ignored quiet promptings, and their paradigms shift accordingly.

The past begins to make new sense, as they reinterpret those annoying doubts and second-guessings as the Lord's gentle proddings. In contrast, those who find their faith unsustainable and so abandon their faith journey, move in the other direction. Those quiet intimations they once took to be God's spirit, those countless minor miracles they took to be answers to prayer, they now interpret as passing moments of self-delusion, wish-fulfillment, and the stuff of mere coincidence.

The point is, neither the new believer nor the new doubter has necessarily progressed or reached enlightenment. Nor has either one necessarily forced the evidence to fit a preconceived model of belief or doubt. Rather, every time we turn our hearts and minds in the direction of giving meaning to our experiences, we are merely—and yet profoundly—arranging the evidence into a pattern—the pattern that makes the most sense to us at a given point on our journey. Evidence does not construct itself into meaningful patterns. That is our work to perform.

In times long past, of course, belief in God was as natural and inevitable as breathing. Up until a few hundred years ago, atheism in the modern sense was unthinkable. The very possibility of skepticism is, within the Christian West at least, of rather recent origin. But the fact is, we now live in a secular age. What this means is that in today's environment, belief in God is an option one chooses among many options. The last century and a half have seen the development of thoroughly secular explanations to account for Christianity, religious yearnings, conscience—even a Creator. For increasing numbers of people, these theories have provided powerful alternatives to traditional belief.

The philosopher Friedrich Nietzsche gave an account of Christianity's invention as a clever ploy by clerics. Resentful at their position at the bottom of the social hierarchy, they convince the high and mighty that weakness is the true virtue, and meekness the most desirable attribute. By so doing, they turn the tables on the rich and powerful, and make themselves—the religious—the morally superior ones. Christianity, in this view, was a brilliant strategy to make a virtue of necessity and reverse society's power dynamics to the advantage of the oppressed.

Sigmund Freud devised influential explanations of the religious impulse as the vague memory of a world we experienced before language, when we had not yet developed a sense of selfhood and still felt at one with the world around us. The feeling of the eternal is therefore simply a buried memory of our infant condition, when we were safely cradled in our mother's arms, before we even thought of ourselves as a being separate and apart from the larger universe. This blissful, if forgotten, sentiment of oneness with the greater world follows us through life, driving our quest for the infinite. As for the figure of God himself, he theorized, He was simply a childish projection of an authoritative father figure. Both Nietzsche and Freud believed humans to be innately aggressive and destructive. Conscience, they theorized, is a mechanism the mind has developed in order to turn our innate impulse toward violence against itself, thereby protecting and preserving society.

With his theory of natural selection, later called "survival of the fittest," Darwin explained how random, incremental change over millions of years, leads to many species developing from one original source, and he proposed mechanisms and processes by which the giraffe acquired his long neck, and our species the miraculous human eye. He seemingly demonstrated that a god is not necessary to account for the plumage of the peacock or the variety of songbirds in the sky. In sum, he made it intellectually respectable to be an atheist. Why, then, do we need faith in God and things eternal?

Perhaps because the development of complex human beings, with self-awareness and lives filled with love and tears and laughter, is one too many a miracle to accept as a purely natural phenomenon. Perhaps because the idea of God is a more reasonable hypothesis than the endless stream of coincidences essential to our origin and existence here on earth: a planet precisely the right distance from the sun, so as to warm but not burn us; a rare, elliptical orbit, combined with just enough tilt to the axis, to give us endurable seasonal change; a nearby moon, of the perfect gravitational size to stabilize our rotation and provide the tides so essential to life's rise; life-sustaining water, that violates the rule (true of other non-metallic substances) whereby it should contract when frozen, thereby *not* causing oceans and lakes to freeze solid from the bottom up; along with a stream of additional universal conditions ranging from the speed of light, to the ratio of protons to electrons, to the gravitational constant, all of which are required to sustain life.

One such coincidence was too much for the astronomer Sir Fred Hoyle. In the 1950s, he discovered that the existence of carbon itself—the basis for life on earth—depended on certain very precise details in nuclear physics. The revelation convinced Hoyle "that the universe was, in his words, 'a put-up job.' For Hoyle, the hand of intelligence had left clear fingerprints all over physics and cosmology." As a result, he reversed "his earlier and vehement anti-God stance."

If those reasons are too rooted in arcane science and arguments about probability, there are other, more accessible evidences for finding belief in God a reasonable choice. Astrophysics may give a credible account of the origin of the stars, and Darwin might explain the development of the human eye, but neither can tell us why the night sky strikes us with soul-piercing quietude, or why our mind aches to understand what is so remote from bodily need.

In addition, "if it really is true that [the human] is merely the inevitable culmination of an improbable chemical reaction . . . involv[ing] 'merely material' atoms, then the fact that he has been able to formulate the idea of 'an improbable chemical reaction' and to trace himself back to it is remarkable indeed. That chemicals which are 'merely material' should come to understand their own nature is a staggering supposition."

Or, to phrase the dilemma another way, as physicist John Polkinghorne writes, "our surplus intellectual capacity, enabling us to comprehend the microworld of quarks and gluons and the macroworld of big bang cosmology, is on such a scale that it beggars belief that this is simply a byproduct of the struggle for life." George Bernard Shaw said it a little differently: "My dog's brain serves only my dog's purposes. But *my* brain labors at a knowledge which does nothing for me personally but make my . . . decay and death a calamity." Put another way, our minds are driven to answer questions that far transcend the bounds of our own lives. The human mind itself is far more powerful and capacious than any instrument necessary for mere self-preservation or the construction of huts or skyscrapers.

We strive to know what transpired in the first moments of the universe, to understand what is happening in black holes and comets across the galaxy, and to envision creation's end when the last sun winks out of existence. Our intelligence does not behave as a mortal thing of time. The best sense we can make out of this riddle is that there is an independent, existing principle of intelligence within us. We believe this intelligence is impelled by an eternal identity and potential to move toward greater understanding of a far larger domain than the place and time of our birth. This is more than an intellectual puzzle to us; we find ourselves in a world where we sense we are more than casual visitors or drive-through patrons. We have a home, an origin, a purpose in mortality, and a future in the cosmos, bound to larger realities than merely natural processes. One of those larger realities toward whom we incline may reasonably be posited as God.

This conclusion seems warranted by another observation. Every craving that we experience finds a suitable object that satisfies and fulfills that longing. Our body hungers; and there is food. We thirst; and there is water. We are born brimming with curiosity; and there is a world to explore and the sensory equipment with which to do so. Other ennobling passions both encompass and transcend bodily longing. We crave intimacy and companionship; and there is human love, as essential to happiness and thriving as any nutrient.

The Greek playwright Aristophanes resorted to myth to explain the all-consuming power of this hunger, but he found his own resolution sadly insufficient. In his story, we existed in a distant past as double-creatures, with two heads, four arms, and four legs. With the strength and power we then possessed, we were tempted to scale heaven and to assault the very gods themselves. We were soundly defeated, and in reprisal, Zeus decided not to annihilate our race but rather to split us all asunder and let us suffer perpetually in our humbled and divided condition. In this severed state of incompleteness, mortal men and women walk the earth.

Aristophanes was surely half-joking, but he captures brilliantly our sense of incompleteness and longing for wholeness, for intimate union with another human being who fits us like our other half. Yet even when we find true love and companionship in the rediscovered other, the restoration that should fulfill us falls short; Aristophanes himself is baffled. It is as if, coming together, we are haunted by the memory of an even more perfect past, when we were even more whole and complete, and this suspicion lends an indefinable melancholy to our present lives. "These are the people who finish out their lives together and still cannot say what it is they want. . . . It's obvious that the soul . . . longs for something else."

So, what can we make of this unsatisfied longing, this sense of a primordial loss that no human love can heal? Aristophanes could not answer the question he posed two and a half millennia ago, but an Anglican poet thought he could. George Herbert replaced the Greek myth with a different creation story—one in which human deficiency was not a curse, but a gentle nudge in God's direction.

When God at first made man,
Having a glasse of blessings standing by;

Let us (said he) poure on him all we can:
Let the world's riches, which dispersed lie,
Contract into a span.
So strength first made a way;
Then beautie flow'd, then wisdome, honour, pleasure:
When almost all was out, God made a stay,
Perceiving that alone of all his treasure
Rest in the bottome lay.
For if I should (said he)
Bestow this jewell also on my creature,
He would adore my gifts in stead of me,
And rest in nature, not the God of Nature:
So both should losers be.
Yet let him keep the rest,
But keep them with repining restlesnesse:
Let him be rich and wearie, that at least,
If goodnesse lead him not, yet wearinesse
May tosse him to my breast.

Herbert was saying in poetry what the early church father Saint Augustine had said more simply: "our hearts are restless till they rest in Thee." Those who place their affections upon God, who find in Him an explanation of our deepest nature, with its self-awareness, its yearnings and strivings, do not find respite from all pain or from all questions. But they do find the only object that seems an adequate match to their infinite desire. Speaking of his own experience with God, the psalmist writes, "He satisfyeth the longing soul, and filleth the hungry soul."

Let us now proceed to a question that often disappears under an assumption. If God exists, does He deserve our worship? We think the question is entirely proper. Augustine reported approvingly that when asked what God was doing before creation, a churchman replied, "getting hell ready for those who pry too deep!" It has seemed self-evident to millions—as it was to Augustine himself—that if God is the author of the universe and all who people it, His status as our rightful Lord and sovereign is beyond any possible doubt. We have no right to question Him, His nature, or His purposes.

But sovereigns, like fathers, can have rightful authority to govern or direct us, with no claim whatsoever on our love—let alone adoration. We cannot prove God exists, and certainly cannot prove that any god who exists is kind and merciful rather than cruel or indifferent. But we can say that only the first type of god is one we would want to worship. We reject out of hand any suggestion that mere cosmic authorship or raw power should itself call forth our loyalty or devotion.

Let us be clear what this means, and what it does not mean. It does not mean we can simply choose the kind of god we want to worship, fashion this ideal god into an idol for our private temple, and assume this fantasy corresponds to anything real in the universe. We cannot create gods that match our desires willy-nilly. But it does mean two things: first, it means some gods are conceivable, both within and outside Christian history, who have no legitimate claim upon us. The Ammonite god Moloch required that adherents sacrifice infants to him by burning them alive. We can reject the worship of such a god without agonizing over our impiety—not because it is unreasonable to *believe* in such a god (though it may be), but because it is unreasonable to *worship* such a god. What of the God Christians have been called upon to worship from time to time?

Augustine believed in a god who had arbitrarily foreordained countless millions to damnation. But he insisted, with curious logic and no hint of protest, that if a child, "at the very outset of its life, is placed under a punishment . . . it has a great good for which to thank its Creator, for the merest beginning of a soul is better than the most perfect material object." He considered any complaint on the subject "slanderous." Some ask, "If it was Adam and Eve who sinned, what did we poor wretches do?" Augustine's ready reply: "My response is brief: let them be silent."

Theologian Peter Abelard agreed, as have countless others, that the very behavior in which God freely indulged, treating His creatures "in whatever way God may wish to," would be "deemed the summit of injustice among men." But that, he concluded, was God's prerogative. French philosopher Blaise Pascal thought nothing could be "more contrary to the rules of our wretched justice than to damn eternally an infant, incapable of volition, for an offense . . . which was committed six thousand years before he was born," yet he embraced "this mystery,—the most incomprehensible of all."

The great reformer Martin Luther wrote a century earlier on the subject of election by grace, saying God "ordains whom, and such as He will, to be receivers and partakers of his preached and offered mercy." And that will, he continues, we have no right to try and understand because it is "the most profound secret of the divine majesty, which He reserves unto Himself and keeps hidden from us." As for exactly why God does not save those it is clearly in His power to save, but rather blames man for what, in Luther's words, we have no power to avoid, "it is not lawful to inquire." This clearly perverse divine will, he concludes, is not to be understood. "It is only to be feared and adored!"

Eighteenth-century church-goers have trembled and generations of school children have wondered at the deity of Jonathan Edwards, whom he described in his classic sermon, "Sinners in the Hands of an Angry God." "The wrath of God," he tells his audience, "is like great waters that are dammed for the present. . . .The God that holds you over the pit of hell, much as one holds a spider, or some loathsome insect over the fire, abhors you." As for the unregenerate, he continues, "When God beholds the ineffable extremity of your case, and sees your torment to be so vastly disproportioned to your strength, and sees how your poor soul is crushed, and sinks down, as it were, into an infinite gloom; He will have no compassion upon you, . . . there shall be no moderation or mercy."

By the nineteenth century, there was growing resistance to this divine tyranny and cosmic injustice. Two forceful examples come not from theology, but from two of the greatest novels of the era. The protagonist of Mark Twain's *Huckleberry Finn* goes through an agony of indecision, faced with the chance to help his friend, the slave Jim, escape his bondage. But, given the laws of the land, and a culture that had little difficulty reconciling slavery and Christianity, Huck fears that by so doing he would offend God. "It would get all around," he fretted,

> that Huck Finn helped a [slave] to get his freedom. . . . The more I studied about this the more my conscience went to grinding me, and the more wicked and low-down and ornery I got to feeling. And at last, when it hit me all of a sudden that here was the plain hand of Providence slapping me in the face and letting me know my wickedness was being watched all the time from up there in heaven. . . . Well, I tried the best I could to kinder soften it up somehow for myself by saying I was brung up wicked, and so I wasn't so much to blame.

At last, he decides to do the "Christian" thing, and turn the slave in. He writes a note betraying Jim, followed by one last pang of remorse. "It was a close place. I took [the note] up, and held it in my hand. I was a-trembling, because I'd got to decide, forever, betwixt two things, and I knowd it. I studied a minute, sort of holding my breath, and then says to myself: 'All right, then, I'll go to hell'—and tore it up." So Huck chooses damnation over the God he was raised to worship.

In Fyodor Dostoyevsky's *The Brothers Karamazov,* the agnostic Ivan makes a similar choice. A sensitive soul, he is wracked by pain at the harrowing accounts he has read of little children who suffer at the hands of savage overseers and cruel parents. He is dissatisfied with a God whose only response to their pain is to punish evil overseers and cruel parents. "What do I care for avenging them?" he cries. "What do I care for a hell for oppressors? . . . I want to forgive. I want to embrace. I don't want more suffering. . . . And so I hasten to give back my entrance ticket, and if I am an honest man I am bound to give it back as soon as possible. And that I am doing. It's not God that I don't accept, Alyosha, only I most respectfully return him the ticket." Any God whose only response to pain and suffering is to inflict more pain and suffering, is not a God Ivan can worship.

Our first point is that if gods such as Moloch, or the God of some Christians, exist, they do not deserve our reverence or our love. We, just as Huck or Ivan or countless others, would be justified in saying, "No, I will not bow to such a God." At the risk of our own eternal annihilation, we would resist. We would not say, with Augustine, that existence under any conditions—including an eternity of undeserved torment—is more to be valued than nonexistence. We do not concede that a god who creates us, or the entire universe for that matter, is beyond reproach or question by virtue of his power alone. We certainly do not accord earthly parents unchallenged prerogatives over their own children, even if they sire, rear, and nourish them.

Our second point is that if we find ourselves inclined to believe a powerful deity does preside over the universe, the assumption that he would be a more perfect embodiment of the morally good that we recognize and seek to emulate is not wishful thinking. Belief in a God who is more rather than less generous and forgiving, who will extend the maximum mercy He can, and impose the minimum justice He must, is not a fanciful hope. It is a logical and reasonable inference. Certainly, this God would be as far above us morally, as He would be intellectually. But it would make sense to look for a

God who inhabits that true north toward which our innate moral compass points us.

For centuries, Christians were told they have no right to expect that their sense of what is just, or true, or right, is a reliable guide to what God considers just, or true, or right. Perhaps, the argument goes, they are simply incapable of understanding Justice, Truth, and the Right writ large, as seen from God's perspective. But we are talking here of more than a simple difference in perspective. Of course our view is partial, and imperfect. The question is, have we good reason to believe we are even in the same ballpark as God when it comes to the values we hold dear? The idea that God's thoughts are not our thoughts, His ways not our ways, has been used as a cudgel to beat into abject submission any who question a Deity's right to save whom He will and damn whom He will, to bless or curse as He chooses, to have His own heavenly notions about what is good and right.

In actual fact, it makes little sense to recognize in our conscience a reliable guide to what is virtuous, lovely, and praiseworthy in the world where God has placed us, while suggesting He inhabits a different moral universe. It makes little sense to insist He endowed us with an intuitive grammar of right and wrong, while He himself speaks a different moral language. As the character in Elie Wiesel's play, *The Trial of God,* protests, if our truth "is not His as well, then He's worse than I thought. Then it would mean that He gave us the taste, the passion of truth without telling us that this truth is not true!"

The biblical story of the Fall indicates, on the contrary, that we are absolutely enmeshed in the same moral order as our God. Whatever momentous change the Garden of Eden story was meant to depict, the author wanted us to know it is not entirely in the direction of sin and loss. One consequence of eating the forbidden fruit, acknowledged by God himself, is a heightened human consciousness—and not just of their nakedness. Adam and Eve became more, not less, like God insofar as they came to see the *same* moral distinctions He did. This was precisely what He confirms, saying Adam and Eve have "become like one of us, knowing good and evil." In all the centuries of Christian hand-wringing and breast-beating that have followed in the wake of the Adamic decision, this fact seems to have disappeared entirely. Humankind and God now share a common moral awareness, a common capacity to judge between right and wrong, a common capacity for love.

Though we may be in the infancy of moral development, as individuals and as a species, surely we are striving toward a perfect model that God already embodies. And while personal and collective progress may be shaky and uneven, some moral imperatives have only grown more sharply defined across time: we reject inhumanity, cruelty, caprice, and callousness. We prize kindness, we value tenderness, and we esteem compassion. Who can doubt the most transcendent instance of human love is a testament to a more perfect source, a love without limit? We are continuing, with tragic and devastating exceptions, on the trajectory inaugurated by Adam and Eve, becoming ever more like God, as we become ever more adept at discerning good and evil, and nourishing the wellsprings of human love. And in so doing, we grow more capable of discerning a kind and merciful God among His many counterfeits.

This tender face of the Divine is too often lost in casual readings of the Old Testament, obscured by the blood and smoke of Canaan's conquest, but it is there to be found. When Moses fears God's patience with a murmuring Israel has expired, he pleads on their behalf. God reassures him, "My presence shall go with thee, and I will give thee rest." We perceive a bond more of intimacy than fear, when Moses replies, "If thy presence go not with me, carry us not up hence." Without your companionship, in other words, the promised land holds no promise, and no appeal. Not to worry, God soothes him. "I know thee by name."

In more recent centuries, some prodigies of conscience have

overleapt centuries of moral darkness to discern a God of great compassion and tenderness, even if it meant swimming against the current. Jonathan Edwards may have terrified thousands with his portrait of an angry God who held sinners over the pit of hell, like loathsome spiders over a flame. But his own wife was drawn to a different version of God. On one occasion when Edwards was out of town, a local preacher named Peter Reynolds came to visit Sarah and her children. He offered to have a prayer with the family, and she agreed. Perhaps, praying in the home of the famous preacher of fire and brimstone, Reynolds entreated God in tones he thought Edwards might have approved. In any event, Sarah was troubled. She recorded in her journal that while the reverend was offering his prayer, she found herself feeling "an earnest desire that, in calling on God, he should say Father." Then she asked herself, "Can *I*, with the confidence of a child, and without the least misgiving of heart, call God my Father?"

Pondering led to yearning. She "felt a strong desire to be alone with God," and withdrew to her chamber. In the moments that followed, "the presence of God was so near, and so real, that I seemed scarcely conscious of anything else. God the Father, and the Lord Jesus Christ, seemed as distinct persons, both manifesting their inconceivable loveliness and mildness, and gentleness, and their great immutable love to me. . . . The peace and happiness, which I hereupon felt, was altogether inexpressible."

Certainly we all, just as Sarah Edwards or Moses, would prefer to worship a God who is merciful and tender in contrast to one who is wrathful and unyielding. But the implications can be troubling, and a moment's reflection suggests why the God of Augustine and Pascal and Luther and Edwards prevailed so long in the minds of so many. Tenderness suggests sensitivity. A loving heart, like an exposed nerve, is by definition susceptible to pain. Do we really want to believe in a God who is thus exposed, unshielded from human sin and evil? Not merely as God incarnate, Jesus of Nazareth, the

Son of Man who suffered, bled, and died—but as God, the Eternal Father, the Everlasting One, the Man of Holiness?

The Christian church's first theologian, Origen, was sure this must be so. "The Father, too, himself, the God of the Universe, 'patient and abounding in mercy' and compassionate, does He not in some way suffer? Or do you not know that when He directs human affairs He suffers human suffering . . . on account of us." Unfortunately, Origen's vision of a suffering God was eventually overwhelmed by the God of the creeds, who lacked "body, parts, and passions." For the suffering God was a possibility that horrified theologians.

The medieval poet Dante, in his graphic masterpiece the *Divine Comedy*, labored to convince his audience that pity of the damned was an unworthy emotion, a rebellion against God's justice. The heaven-dwelling saint Beatrice explains why she is unmoved by the sufferings of the damned she sees all about her: "God, in his graciousness, has made me so that this, your misery, cannot touch me." In this view, God's unresponsiveness to the torments of the wicked is both a divine model worthy of emulation and a gift bestowed on the righteous (and goes a very long way to explain how generations of Christians could in good conscience blithely consign legions of heretics to agonizing deaths at the stake).

Even C. S. Lewis was sure of a future when love could no longer exact the desperate price it now does. In the heaven he imagines, one of the saved is pestered by her former lover, seeking pity in his misery. She responds, "Did you think joy was created to live always under that threat? . . . Can you really have thought that love and joy would always be at the mercy of frowns and sighs? . . . Your darkness cannot now infect the light." What is true of lovers, Lewis intimates, is also true of God. To imagine a God literally troubled or grieving for His wayward creatures would be monstrous in this view, because it would make God hostage to the whims of those creatures. His perfect peace could be disturbed by the "wicked"; the darkness could "infect the light."

The problem of vulnerability wrought by love was precisely the point made by the essayist Francis Bacon and by the psychologist Freud. "He that hath wife and children hath given hostages to fortune," wrote Bacon. "We are never so defenseless against suffering as when we love," said Freud. The novelist Graham Greene's wise but flawed priest learns the same lesson, encountering his young daughter: "He was aware of an immense load of responsibility: it was indistinguishable from love."

Is God hostage in some way to His limitless love? What is the nature of God's responsibility toward the human family? The whole matter of God's involvement with human concerns appears at times an unfathomable mystery. "Look at the heavens," Elihu challenges a bewildered, suffering Job, "and see; observe the clouds which are higher than you. If you have sinned, . . . if your transgressions are multiplied, what do you do to him? If you are righteous, what do you give to him?"

With these questions, scripture shatters any comfortable assumptions we may draw from deity's relationship to the human, the expectation that God owes us blessings when we are good and that He will inevitably punish us when we are not. Surely, if a neighbor appeared at our door informing us he had fed the poor and expected our gratitude, we would be puzzled. And if a colleague approached us with a confession that he had cheated on his taxes and awaited our punishment, we would consider him deranged. Whence comes the expectation, Elihu is asking, that God should have some inherent interest in our actions, good or evil?

Israel's covenant with God presupposes some kind of mutual relationship. And yet with God, what reciprocity can exist? What possible reason could we have to expect reward for righteousness? What possible rationale can God have for noticing our sinfulness? What grounds have we to expect He should care at all? These rhetorical questions all converge in a thunderous, if unexpressed, "none." But humans and their world *do* matter to God. Why that should be, the Psalmist could no more fathom than Elihu. He asked in comparable amazement, "What are human beings that you are mindful of them, mortals that you care for them? Yet you have made them a little lower than God, and crowned them with glory and honor."

The answer to Elihu's query, the astounding mystery of our relationship to the Divine, had actually been revealed in the very question a baffled Job had posed earlier. "What is man, that thou shouldest magnify him? and that thou shouldest set thine heart upon him?" The astonishing revelation here is that God *does set His heart upon us*. And in so doing, God *chooses* to love us. And if love means responsibility, sacrifice, vulnerability, then God's decision to love us is the most stupendously sublime moment in the history of time. He chooses to love even at, necessarily at, the price of vulnerability.

It is God's response to the manifold creatures by whom He is surrounded, the movement of His heart and will in the direction of those other beings—us—that becomes *the* defining moment in His Godliness, and establishes the pattern of His divine activity. His freely made choice to inaugurate and sustain costly loving relationships *is* the very core of His divine identity.

The most remarkable religious document published in the nineteenth century may well be an ascension narrative in which the prophet Enoch is taken into heaven and records his ensuing vision. He sees Satan's dominion over the earth, and God's unanticipated response to a world veiled in darkness: "The God of heaven looked upon the residue of the people, and He wept; and Enoch bore record of it, saying: How is it that the heavens weep, and shed forth their tears as the rain upon the mountains? And Enoch said unto the Lord: How is it that thou *canst* weep?"

The question here is not about the reasons behind God's tears. Enoch does not ask, *why* do you weep, but rather, *how are your tears even possible*, "seeing thou art holy, and from all eternity to all eternity?" Clearly, Enoch, who believed God to be "merciful and kind forever," did not expect such a being could be moved to the point of distress by the sins of His children. And so a third time he asks, "how *is it* thou *canst* weep?"

The answer, it turns out, is that God is not exempt from emotional pain. Exempt? On the contrary, God's pain is as infinite as His love. He weeps because He feels compassion. As the Lord explains to Enoch, "unto thy brethren have I said, and also given commandment, that they should love one another, and that they should choose me, their Father; but behold, they are without affection, and they hate their own blood . . . and misery shall be their doom; and the whole heavens shall weep over them, even all the workmanship of mine hands; wherefore should not the heavens weep, seeing these shall suffer?"

It is not their wickedness, but their "misery," not their disobedience, but their "suffering," that elicits the God of Heaven's tears. Not until Gethsemane and Golgotha does the scriptural record reveal so unflinchingly the costly investment of God's love in His people, the price at which He placed His heart upon them. There could be nothing in this universe, or in any possible universe, more perfectly good, absolutely beautiful, worthy of adoration, and deserving of emulation, than this God of love and kindness and vulnerability. That is why a gesture of belief in His direction, a decision to acknowledge His virtues as the paramount qualities of a divided universe, is a response to the best in us, the best and noblest of which the human soul is capable. A God without body or parts is conceivable. But a God without passions would engender in our hearts neither love nor interest. In the vision of Enoch, we find ourselves drawn to a God who prevents all the pain He can, assumes all the suffering He can, and weeps over the misery He can neither prevent nor assume.

This motif of the weeping God appears in other ancient

traditions. In one Talmudic text, the passage made famous by Handel's *Messiah* is markedly recast to suggest that God, burdened by the sins of the world, appeals to His people to console *Him*, not the other way around. "Comfort *me*, comfort *me*, my people," the text reads. As early as the days of Noah, the pain of humankind "grieved him to his heart." In this connection, it is significant that the God of the Old Testament asks His people to "make *me* a sanctuary, so that I may dwell among them." In other words, the temple Solomon builds, like the tabernacle in the wilderness, is *God's* sanctuary and place of refuge, not ours. For a being as good and pure as God to enter into this realm of darkness and depravity must be exquisitely painful on every level. His love impels Him to visit His people in their distress, and the temple is His shield and refuge from the full onslaught of worldly pain and evil.

God's love is not metaphorical. It is not some impersonal analogue to the compassion we experience. Compassion, in its root meaning, signifies "to suffer with, or alongside." In the story of Job, before his friends turn into miserable counselors, they are sublime examples of compassionate friendship. Job's loss of family and wealth has been compounded by disease so severe it disfigures him to the point of nonrecognition. The story continues,

> Now when Job's three friends heard of all these troubles that had come upon him, each of them set out from his home—Eliphaz the Temanite, Bildad the Shuhite, and Zophar the Naamathite. They met together to go and console and comfort him. When they saw him from a distance, they did not recognize him, and they raised their voices and wept aloud; they tore their robes and threw dust in the air upon their heads. They sat with him on the ground seven days and seven nights, and no one spoke a word to him.

For a full week of days and nights, Job's friends do what genuine friends are called to do: their actions seem little enough, but they are sublimely great. They "suffer with"; they participate in Job's anguish. This human capacity to suffer pain at the distress of a loved one is an imperfect shadow of the unfathomable grief a perfect being feels when His creations put themselves beyond His healing embrace. Some early Christians were sure even Satan never fell outside the orbit of a merciful Father and would one day be returned to fellowship. At the very least, a modern revelation declares that when Lucifer, Son of the Morning, rebelled against his God he was called "Perdition, for the heavens wept over him." If the heavens wept over Lucifer at his fall, how much more must God's heart beat in sympathy with those children whose presence on earth is proof they are neither rebels nor exiles from His love.

Divine vulnerability is most dramatically embodied in the figure and mission of the Christ. Jesus Christ has had unparalleled hold on the human heart because He fully shared in the human condition, a "glorious, yet contracted light" that "stole into a manger" in order to experience the entire sordid and suffering span of the human condition. The story of His life and ministry strikes us with wonder for two reasons. First, it establishes a real, shared intimacy that only fellow travelers in suffering can know. "In all their affliction, He was afflicted," wrote Isaiah. Christ's life in the flesh gave Him an empathy transcending the theoretical. Taking upon Himself human infirmities, "His bowels" were indeed "filled with mercy, according to the flesh, that He may know according to the flesh how to succor His people according to their infirmities."

Christ's empathy then is not some inherent attribute of the Divine. It was dearly paid for, each day of His mortal life, filled as it was with all the trauma an uncomprehending world could inflict on perfect innocence. He knew the physical rigors of hunger and thirst, and the emotional deserts of loneliness and rejection. But perfect empathy would have to go beyond a life that simply paralleled our own, or that entailed only the particulars of His private, harrowing journey.

Emily Dickinson contemplated the pains of her own reclusive, burdened life, which paled to the point of nothingness when she compared them to Christ's final friendlessness:

I SHALL know why, when time is over,
And I have ceased to wonder why;
Christ will explain each separate anguish
In the fair schoolroom of the sky.
He will tell me what Peter promised,
And I, for wonder at his woe,
I shall forget the drop of anguish
That scalds me now, that scalds me now.

Peter, of course, had promised Jesus he would never leave His side, never deny, never forsake Him. Yet before Christ endured the first of His physical tortures, His friends had fled, and the chief of His disciples had abandoned Him to face the night of horror alone. Dickinson saw her anguish as mere drops in the infinite sea of the suffering Christ's loneliness. But it was not just His friends who deserted Him. To have an endless empathy, He would have to know a terror and abandonment and hopelessness beyond human conceiving, such that no mortal tongue could say, you don't know what I have known, you haven't been where I have been. Exactly how this would be possible, who can say, but that is what He would have to experience.

So at the close of His life, He hung on the cross to die, with no angels to sing Him home, no light shining at the far end of the tunnel. "I have trodden the wine press alone." Who can imagine the oblivion into which He peered, the suffocating gloom, the infinite void? He who was present on Creation's morn, the Light of the World, now faced a darkness beyond any night. And then, at the acme of His agony, He was sundered from the only solace in His pain-racked life, the only constant comfort in His suffering—His

Father's presence. The shock and horror of that final, insupportable abandonment is heard in His cry of despair, "My God, my God, why have *you* forsaken me?"

The story of Christ's life amazes for a second reason: it tells us something about a particular power only made manifest in vulnerability. The paradox of Christ's saving sway is that it operates on the basis of what the world would call weakness. Christ aimed to "draw all men unto" Himself by His ignominious crucifixion, not His triumphant resurrection. We are drawn to the suffering Christ, *not* the victorious Christ. As the Christian martyr to Nazism Dietrich Bonhoeffer wrote a friend, "The Bible directs man to God's powerlessness and suffering; only the suffering God can help. . . . The God of the Bible . . . wins power and space in the world by his weakness."

This is the kind of vulnerability betokened by Ruth, the Moabite woman. Widowed and a Gentile, without prospects in her homeland, she devotes herself to her mother-in-law, Naomi, faithfully following her home to Bethlehem. There, an impoverished Ruth gleans grain in the fields of the wealthy landowner and distant relative of Naomi, Boaz. Seeing that Ruth has caught the notice of her kinsman, Naomi instigates a plan whereby Ruth can secure a marriage with him. Her plan is more than risky; it is potentially catastrophic.

Ruth enters into the threshing barn of the sleeping Boaz in the dead of night and by so doing, places herself in a hopelessly compromising situation with hazard to her reputation and life. She is foreign-born with no friend or protector, and no alibi, no story to tell a public, if Boaz simply wakes up and exploits the situation for his own advantage. Not a practice we would want our daughters to follow, but neither would we advocate our young son face a hostile giant without armor, without shield. The point in both cases is for us is to discern the moral in the apparent madness, the purpose behind such conspicuous risk.

The marvel, of course, is that the sole immediate purpose of

Ruth's actions is to make herself vulnerable. Vulnerability *is* her end. Her only objective is to make herself as exposed and defenseless as she can, so she can say to Boaz, "I am Ruth, your servant; spread your cloak over your servant." In other words, here am I, yours to protect or destroy. I place myself in your hands. I hold nothing back, so you may know my trust is without bounds. But of course, in making herself so vulnerable, she reveals the exquisite beauty of her own character. "May you be blessed by the Lord, my daughter," an awestruck Boaz responds. "For all the assembly of my people know that you are a worthy woman." Worthy enough that Ruth, the woman from Moab, becomes a mother in Israel, ancestress of David the King, and of Christ the Lord.

We hear echoes here of another person, similarly made vulnerable, similarly blessed of the Lord—the mother of Christ herself. This time, no mother-in-law, but the angel Gabriel, directs a young woman, telling Mary she shall conceive a son. How can this be, Mary asks, since I am unwed, and a virgin? At this moment, we come to see that Christmas was rather different on the far side of our celebrations. Jesus' nativity was our occasion for joy, but the Coventry Carol reminds us that even His birth came at a dreadful cost.

Herod the King, in his raging,
Charged he hath this day;
His men of might, in his own sight,
All children young, to slay.
Then woe is me, poor Child, for Thee,
And ever mourn and say;
For Thy parting, nor say nor sing,
By, by, lully, lullay

The holiest of nights redounded in terror for the mothers of "Bethlehem and in all the borders thereof." So too was the annunciation itself a cause for angels to sing, but also for a young maiden to tremble with fear. She is perplexed by the angel's visit. Gabriel responds, Fear not. He knows full well the terrible weight he is about to place upon her. For Mary, little more than a girl, is asked to subject herself to an unwed pregnancy, in circumstances beyond any possibility of understanding. She will face the certain prospects of dishonor, public humiliation, and possible death by stoning. Surely with more terror than delight, she replies, "Here am I, the servant of the Lord; let it be with me according to your word." As with Ruth, the next recorded words she hears are "Blessed are you among women."

Ruth, David, Mary—all esteemed progenitors of the Christ—are also types and symbols of His own offering. Only by opening themselves to the possibility of paramount harm to themselves, do they serve as vehicles of His grace. That vulnerability is both the price of the power to save, and that which saves. Luke records an instance when, in the press of a crowd, Jesus detects that someone has touched the tassel of His garment, and asks who it was. He is being jostled and bumped from every side and direction, says a baffled Peter, and He wants to know who touched Him? But someone did more than touch. She drew from Him a healing power. And He felt it flow out of Him. In this scene, too, we discern a greater meaning. Christ's power to heal comes at a cost to Him. As Herbert wrote,

> *Not sealed, but with open eyes*
> *I fly to thee, and fully understand*
> *. . . at what rate and price I have thy love.*

Whatever other meanings we may impute to Christ's crucifixion, it was an act of ultimate self-surrender, the culminating scene of a sacrifice in which nothing was held back. This supernal act of vulnerability invited His own destruction, even as it drew millions to Him. It was Ruth's exposure to risk that won the heart of Boaz.

When Mary accepted a position of peril, she showed herself worthy to nurture the Christ child. That which made Christ's death possible, also made it infinitely efficacious. God "wins power . . . *by* his weakness," Bonhoeffer said. Only the remoteness of Golgotha in space and time, our dim and partial vision of its infinite cost, gives us now the freedom to respond with a heart that inclines or a heart that retreats.

Such weakness and the love behind Christ's sacrifice cannot be bracketed as a unique act of condescension, supernal as it was. This vulnerability, this openness to pain and exposure to risk, *is* the eternal condition of the Divine. That was Enoch's amazed discovery. The suffering that Gethsemane and Golgotha signified cannot be relegated neatly to one of God's modes or persons. It was not just as the embodied Christ that He was "afflicted in all their afflictions." The shadow of the cross is long enough to heal the past and anticipate the future, but whatever the philosophers say, God does not exist outside time. He is not some cosmic ventriloquist, or a magic jack-in-the box, assuming human form once or twice a thousand years to speak, then reverting back to ineffable substance, now popping back into a human universe to interact with His creations.

We may inhabit realms as different as those of fish and fowl; we may swim while He soars, and breathe a different air. But when God speaks from heaven, or His angels minister, a wing breaks the water and heaven and the sea touch. We share the same universe, the same existence that continues through time. God's love, His vulnerability, are a permanent condition of who He is. For God the Father, as for the Son, whatever power or influence He wields over the hearts of men, it is not the power or influence known to the world. Neither here nor hereafter will God exert "control or dominion or compulsion upon the souls of the children of men." God draws men to heaven "by long-suffering, by gentleness and meekness, and by love unfeigned; By kindness, and pure knowledge." His realm of influence is everlasting, but "without compulsory means it [flows unto him] forever and ever."

• • •

If vulnerability and pain are the price of love, then joy is its reward. That was the lesson Adam and Eve learn in the Garden, but the principle was rooted in the heavens. As surely as the dark gives meaning to the dawn, so does pain give meaning to pleasure, and sorrow to joy. All that we love, all that we strive for, all that we relish, we know only by contrast. The lesson of Creation is that the world acquires its meaning only through differentiation. It is in separating the light from the darkness, that God's work of the first day is complete. And so He continues day by day, making a distinction between what is of the heavens, and what is of the earth, where the water flows, and where the land begins, the domain of the stars and the province of the moon. And He pronounces His work complete, only when He separates the man and woman, then draws them back together in a relationship of mutuality that gives vitality and fruitfulness to what is human. All that exists in our world of meaning must exist in paired opposition.

In the Garden story, good and evil are found on the same tree, not in separate orchards. Good and evil give meaning and definition to each other. If God, like us, is susceptible to immense pain, He is, like us, the greater in His capacity for happiness. The presence of such pain serves the larger purposes of God's master plan, which is to maximize the human capacity for joy, or in other words, "to bring to pass the immortality and eternal life of man." He can no more foster those ends in the absence of suffering and evil than one could find the traction to run or the breath to sing in the vacuum of space. God does not instigate pain or suffering, but He can weave it into His purposes. "God's power rests not on totalizing omnipotence, but on His ability to alchemize suffering, tragedy, and loss into wisdom, understanding, and joy."

Even more abundantly than His sharing in human sorrows, we find evidence of God's delight in human happiness. There is the sense in Old Testament scripture that Creation itself is an overflowing of God's own joyfulness. In Proverbs 8, a personified Wisdom sings of a moment, "before the beginning of the earth," when she was witness to God's designs. "When he marked out the foundations of the earth, then I was beside him, . . . and I was daily his delight, rejoicing before him always, rejoicing in his inhabited world and delighting in the human race."

The Lord Himself describes for Job His laying of the earth's foundations, as a moment "when the morning stars sang together and all the heavenly beings shouted for joy." It is as if God's own nature spills over, and His gladness multiplies through a progeny that will share in His own capacity for joyful activity and love-filled relationships. In a more recent scripture, Christ proclaims that this was His purpose all along, and His central, even His only concern. For "He doeth not anything save it be for the benefit of the world; for he loveth the world."

The motif of a joy so abundant it required the creation of a world to accommodate it is manifest in the same overabundance that fills all creation. Jesus told the multitudes, "I came that they may have life, and have it abundantly (περισσὸν)." The key Greek word here is *perissone*, which means "full to overflowing"; "present in superabundance." God is a God of superabundance, as described by the poet Robinson Jeffers:

Is it not by his high superfluousness we know
Our God? For to be equal a need
Is natural, . . . : but to fling
Rainbows over the rain
And beauty above the moon, and secret rainbows

On the domes of deep sea-shells,
And make the necessary embrace of breeding
Beautiful also as fire,
Not even the weeds to multiply without blossom
Nor the birds without music. . . .

The naturalist Joseph Wood Krutch thought it was this very song of the birds that demonstrated an excess, a redundancy in nature. Birds sing to warn of danger, or to attract a mate. But they also sing for joy. One biologist has written, "To be a bird is to be alive more intensely than any other living creature, man included. . . . They live in a world that is always the present, mostly full of joy." Joy itself is not necessary, useful, or productive to the workings of the natural world. In a universe limited by the economy of the essential, joy is proof of a surplus. In the grueling contest for survival, amidst the grind of animal existence, endowed with the biological machinery best adapted for reproducing his species, what time or need has the robin for inessential music? The song of the bird, like the joy of a human, is not a passive acquiescence to what is, an acceptance of the conditions of life. It is an energy-infused celebration of that life, a recognition of its giftedness.

The human body and human soul alike seem to be constituted by their Maker for the amassing of experience in ever greater variety and intensity. A dog or a carrion-eating bird will ingest anything capable of sustaining its beating heart one more day. But the human palate is refined enough to register infinite grades of difference among fine wines. Our sense of smell strikes us as almost entirely superfluous, since we don't need it to hunt prey or be alerted to danger—but it does register the difference between a rose and a lily, the aroma of Christmas pine and fresh-baked bread, and it lets us know when we have escaped the smog of the city and can relish the cleansing air of the country. If we are made in God's image, we can see His joyful nature reflected in the arsenal of access He gave us, to a variegated world of color and sound and texture and taste and smell.

Darwin was sure that even those spectacles of nature that overwhelm us by their beauty, from the peacock's tail to the fragrance of an English rose, serve not man's purpose but their own, which is survival and reproducibility. If anything in nature could be found that had been "created for beauty in the eyes of man" rather than the good of its possessor, it would be "absolutely fatal" to his theory. In other words, maple leaves in autumn do not suddenly transform into stained glass pendants, illuminated by a setting sun, in order to satisfy a human longing for beauty. Their scarlet, ochre, and golden colors emerge as chlorophyll production shuts down, in preparation for sacrificing the leaves that are vulnerable to winter cold, and ensuring the survival of the tree. But the tree survives, *while* our vision is ravished. The peacock's display attracts a hen, *and* it nourishes the human eye. The flower's fragrance entices a pollinator, *but it also* intoxicates the gardener. In that "while," in that "and," in that "but it also," we find the giftedness of life.

Therein lies the most telling sign of a vast superabundance. Nature's purposes and God's purposes are not in competition but work in tandem. If the first works by blind necessity, the second works by generosity. And in recognizing that giftedness, we turn from appreciation to gratitude; from admiration for the world's efficiency and order, to love of its beauty and grandeur. This movement is captured in the life of Wayne Booth, one of America's greatest literary critics. He lost his faith in God as a young man, and then recovered at least a portion of it in his last years. A friend spoke at his memorial service and related one of his last conversations with the ailing scholar. "I had brought him lunch, and as we sat at the table sunlight fell upon a crystal in [his wife] Phyllis's collection, scattering patches of rainbow color over the walls and ceiling. 'There!' said Wayne, 'don't you feel grateful?' 'It's beautiful,' I said, 'and it makes me happy, but I don't feel grateful. I wish I did. I'm glad that you do.'"

The difference between these two men, between appreciation of beauty, and feeling gratitude for that beauty, is the recognition of an agent *behind* the beauty. A person responsible for creating something admirable and delightsome, towards whom we feel love and appreciation. Booth's friend understood this difference. As he explained, "Wayne's . . . relation with this God was personal. . . . One of gratitude, gratitude for all that is good and beautiful." Gratitude is an illogical response to a world that never had us in mind as an audience; but it is the fitting tribute to an original Creator who anticipated our joy and participates fully in it.

As the scripture says, "the beasts of the field and the fowls of the air, and that which climbeth upon the trees and walketh upon the earth; . . . Yea, all things which come of the earth, in the season thereof, are made for the benefit and the use of man, both to please the eye and to gladden the heart; Yea, for food and for raiment, for taste and for smell, to strengthen the body and to enliven the soul. *And it pleaseth God that He hath given all these things unto man.*"

God's desire, so manifest in the texture of the created order, is to enlarge the sphere of human joy, and we discover the marvelous truth that our joy is His joy. What greater motivation could there be for us to seek out and secure our own, our friends', our families' happiness, than to know it adds to His. Truly, God has made us His central concern, and as long as humans live—He will share in all our sorrows. But He also shares in all our triumphs and joys. For He has set His heart upon us.

CHAPTER TWO

Man Was in the Beginning with God

We lived as spirit beings in the presence of God before we were born into this mortal life.

"He has put eternity in their hearts, without which man cannot discover God."

Let me but be taught the mystery of my being," pleads one of Lord Byron's characters, in tones the apostle Paul would have readily understood. Paul wrote a beautiful hymn to charity, which the King James translators rendered in part, "For now we see through a glass darkly." By "glass" they meant a looking glass, a mirror. The original actually reads, "We see in a mirror, dimly" (NRSV). In other words, *we* are the mystery yet to be revealed. It is our *own* identity that we must struggle to discern, before we can rightly perceive our place in the cosmos and our relation to the Divine. With the poet John Keats we feel to say, "Do you not think I strive—to know myself?" And like him, we find ourselves, "straining at particles of light in the midst of a great darkness." Straining because we never feel completely at home in this world and because we sense we carry within us clues to our origins. We experience those sparks in the night as though we were archaeologists glimpsing familiar fragments of our lost culture, not relics of an alien world. It is more than the recurrent intimations of a different sphere, a different domain of existence only dimly perceived, that haunt us. It is the familiarity we cannot shake, which tells us as much about ourselves as about those realms beyond the veil that shrouds our life in mystery.

Among the ancient Babylonians, Greeks, Romans, Jews, and early Christians, many believed the premortal life of the soul made powerful sense of myriad puzzles. Christians especially asked, "Might memory explain the turn of the longing soul toward God?" Scores of poets, philosophers, and clerics have thought it does. "My own experience is rather 'devastating desire'—desire for that-of-which-the-present-joy-is-a-reminder. All my life nature and art have been *reminding* me of something I've never seen: saying 'Look! What does this—and this—remind you of?'" writes C. S. Lewis. He was simply paraphrasing St. Augustine, who was similarly haunted by the suspicion that the longing in his soul was a pining for a past happiness. "How then do I seek You?" Augustine asks. "For in seeking You, my God, it is happiness I am seeking." But how can that be possible? "Where and when had I any experience of happiness, that I should remember it and love it and long for it?" Clearly, those who seek God and the happy life He represents must "have known it," though "I know not how," he considers. The woman of the parable who lost her coin gives him a clue, for she "would not have found it if she had not remembered it. . . . It was lost only to the eyes; it was preserved in memory." So it must be with God, he reasons. "How shall I find You if I am without memory of you?" We can only seek what we have known, and knowledge of God, then, must be *memory* of God.

A few centuries earlier, Augustine's fellow churchman Clement of Alexandria had made a similar argument. To repent, he argued, is to turn from the life we know to another concealed in shadow. Only a reminiscence of "better things," vaguely perceived, could be a sufficient prompt to make us renounce present certainties, with their satisfactions and pleasures, for something better. In turning to God, therefore, we are not converting—but *re*verting—to a holy model, "speed[ing] back to the eternal light, children to the Father."

The sense that we are pilgrims in a strange land is one of the most universal themes in human culture. No argument can persuade, or logic confound, where our deepest feeling is the foundation. For William Wordsworth, the intimation of a prior existence was overwhelming—a "presence which is not to be put by." He famously wrote that "heaven lies about us in our infancy" for the simple reason that "our birth is but a sleep and a forgetting. The soul that riseth with us, our life's star, hath had elsewhere its setting, and cometh from afar. Not in entire forgetfulness, and not in utter nakedness, but trailing clouds of glory do we come from God who is our home." His colleague, Samuel Coleridge, moved by the contemplation of his infant son, similarly wondered if "we liv'd, ere yet this robe of flesh we wore?" He defended his feelings as more than poetic fancy when he wrote later to a friend, "if you never have had [intimations of preexistence] yourself, I cannot explain [them] to you."

In this view of human identity, the restlessness in human nature, which Herbert described, is not a deliberate deficiency bestowed by the creator. It is a simple longing for our true home, a "groping after our own Centre's near and proper substance." As Amos Bronson Alcott wrote, "All unrest is but the struggle of the soul to reassure herself of her inborn immortality; Her discomfort reveals . . . her loss of the divine presence."

Who has never felt the utter inadequacy of the world to satisfy the spiritual longings of our nature? Why the heart's persistent inkling that we are adrift from our origins? Why such easy agreement with the poet's picture of a "soul, uneasy and confined from home?" Why are we so ready to lament with the dramatist that we have been set "naked and miserable upon the shores of this great ocean of the world?" The insatiable longing for wholeness described in the myth of Aristophanes, finds myriad echoes in the centuries since. In Frances Cornford's poem, "Preexistence," the poet gives expression to what many have felt:

I laid me down upon the shore
And dreamed a little space;
I heard the great waves break and roar;
The sun was on my face.

. . .

The grains of sand so shining-small
Soft through my fingers ran;
The sun shone down upon it all,
And so my dream began:
How all of this had been before:
How ages far away
I lay on some forgotten shore
As here I lie today.

. . .

I have forgotten whence I came,
Or what my home might be,
Or by what strange and savage name
I called that thundering sea.
I only know the sun shone down
As still it shines today,
And in my fingers long and brown
The little pebbles lay.

One theologian found in premortal existence a solution to "the mystery of that inextinguishable melancholy and sadness, which lies hidden at the foundation of all human consciousness, being most profound in the noblest natures. The lower animals," he noted, "are light and joyous, content if their actual wants are supplied, secure and untroubled from without. But in the consciousness of man . . . amid the sounds of heartiest joy there runs an unsilenced undertone of secret sadness. . . . Its existence can be traced back beyond the confines of time."

Reason lends weight to haunting suspicions. We know things we have never learned. One does not need to be a Mozart prodigy to encounter this mystery. The poet/artist William Blake was convinced that his mind was filled with "books & pictures of old, which I wrote & painted in ages of Eternity before my mortal life." More commonly, yet sublimely, we are born with a moral compass, a sense of the beautiful, a capacity to respond to what is best and noblest in human nature. Marcel Proust wrote of this sense that

> everything is arranged in this life as though we entered it carrying the burden of obligations contracted in a former life; there is no reason inherent in the conditions of life on this earth that can make us consider ourselves obliged to do good, to be fastidious, to be polite even. . . . All these obligations which have not their sanction in our present life seem to belong to a different world, founded upon kindness, scrupulosity, self-sacrifice, a world entirely different from this, which we leave in order to be born into this world, before perhaps returning to the other to live once again beneath the sway of those unknown laws which we have obeyed because we bore their precepts in our hearts.

A sudden insight illuminates the mind, words resonate like chords of memory swept by an invisible hand, and we know a new truth as an old one. The music is familiar, even if we have forgotten the words. "Seeds of light, . . . scatter'd in the Soul of Man," one seventeenth-century philosopher called these ornaments of the spirit, which we bring with us when we acquire "the veil of Sense." An eternal soul, one that stretches as endlessly into the past as the future, makes sense of much that an abrupt entry upon the world's stage cannot.

For example, how can we be stirred by our sense of the eternal, how could we even resonate to such music, if we were not tuned to the same scale? Something analogous to the pre-wired mind is going on. Psychologists and linguists have long asserted that babies are born with their brains pre-programmed to learn languages, or music, or other skills. It is as if the human computer has all the software already installed. This is one way of explaining the infant's phenomenal capacity to acquire linguistic or musical proficiency with such astounding ease and rapidity. They already "get" the idea of language when months old, acquire the entire grammar from spoken samples, and plug in vocabulary at the rate of dozens of words a week until fluent. (Try learning Mandarin that way at the age of fifty!)

In a more fundamental way, we are pre-wired to speak the language of the Spirit. Our powers of reason and sense don't give us access to many things that lie beyond the physical. Yet we recognize and respond to this larger realm we call the infinite, the eternal, the holy, or the sacred. How odd that such intimations strike us, not as the babble of a foreign tongue, but as a song heard long ago—"church bells beyond the stars heard." We may think that the spiritual intimations Wordsworth describes are necessary to conclude there was premortal existence. But it may be the other way around. It may be that premortal existence best explains why we are able to respond to spiritual intimations in the first place. We bring the grammar of sacred things with us.

We are also, most of us at least, possessed of a suspicion that we have an identity that lies deeper than our body, rooted beyond actions, reaching past memory. "I . . . have the intuition," writes a contemporary philosopher, "that I—this very self—might have been born of different parents, indeed as a different species of animal. And this intuition is very strong with me; I think it is sound. If it is, then that very fact may imply that my birth and my beginning are two different things."

In other words, if you can say meaningfully, "If I had been born in Calcutta," then you are presupposing a someone or something that existed before your birth, and might have been born in one place as well as another, but took up its earthly home where your birth certificate indicates. Such a hypothetical statement could never be a proof of preexistence. But the ease and naturalness with which we all can say such things is evidence of a deep, even unaware, assumption on our part that we exist as something that precedes and transcends the particular form in which we find ourselves at the moment.

The novelist and essayist Marilynne Robinson has referred to the "odd privilege of existence as a coherent self, . . . that haunting I who wakes us in the night wondering where time has gone, the I we waken to, sharply aware that we have been unfaithful to ourselves." We all know the sensation of having failed to live up to who we are—the sense that there exists a different "I" than the one that sometimes manifests itself through our actions. This perception is ingrained in our very language of self-justification. "I wasn't myself," we might say. Or, "you are better than that," a friend or relative might tell us after a disappointing course of conduct.

Who is this "I" we are referring to in such instances? It could just be an idealized self we have in mind, except the sense is too strong that it is our actions that are unreal, not the self to which we compare them. So, is the most plausible candidate for that "I" really a hypothetical self we might someday be, or is it what the minister and novelist George MacDonald called an "old soul," a self with a long history, that provides the contrast with present patterns of behavior?

The stuff of our physical bodies is almost immeasurably old. "We are made of material created and ejected into the Galaxy by the violence of earlier stars," writes one physicist. "The iron atoms in our blood carrying oxygen at this moment to our cells came largely from exploding white dwarf stars, while the oxygen itself came mainly from exploding supernovas . . . and most of the carbon . . . came from planetary nebulas, the death clouds of middle-size stars."

Surprisingly, a poet and churchman writing over three centuries ago recognized this same fact. Before it acquired its present form, he wrote, the stuff of which the body is made was "in places unimaginably distant," and has traveled "through the triangular passages of as many Vortices as we see Stars in a clear frosty night, and has shone once as bright as the Sun . . . insomuch that we eat, and drink, and cloath our selves with that which was once pure Light and Flame." One could hardly accord our paltry mortal shell a greater or more ancient legacy than the soul it houses, he thought. Both, it would seem, "do bear the same date with the Creation of the World."

If an origin among the stars is difficult to believe, an existence thought to commence with our mortal birth has its own absurdities to contend with. Many beginnings may be inauspicious, but they should at least bear the seeds of future glories. True enough, butterflies and swans come from crawling caterpillars and unremarkable goslings, but the finished product is all present in their beginnings. They may be invisible to the naked eye, but the delicate wings and downy feathers, are all present at their conception. But what are we to say about human beings? That a paltry creature, an anonymous urchin, may grow into a Shakespeare, a Newton, or a Mother Teresa is miracle enough. Shall we also claim the destiny of an eternal being, for a babe that springs into existence by mere happenstance?

There is an almost intolerable lack of sober reflection, foresight, and design behind most human conception. Life begins by chance, by accident, by violence or by carelessness. The young, the frivolous, the unworthy, and the thoughtless can engender a child. And yet the product engendered is one we recognize as something majestic, touched with divinity, and endowed with immortality. "It certainly seems questionable to expect such a powerful effect from such inconsequential causes," mused the great philosopher Immanuel Kant. There must be a true beginning rooted in a time and place of greater dignity and moment. How much more reasonable, it would seem, to posit an origin commensurate with our future, to place our soul's true birth, like its potential destiny, in divine realms.

One might object that the most valuable thing in the world, human life, can be terminated by chance or whim. If one can end a priceless human life through a careless gesture, why could one not engender a priceless human soul the same way? The answer, it would seem, is that termination of life is actually transition. To take a life is to send the soul to another place. We can destroy the body, but not the soul. So, too, it seems reasonable, we can clothe a soul with flesh, but cannot create the soul itself. In both cases, we have the power to aid in a stage of the soul's progress through time, but neither to begin nor end it. How much more consistent it is to contemplate a human identity that extends eternally in both directions, a human existence marked by incremental progress like a continuous line, rather than an abrupt beginning and endless future like a ray, or a flash of aborted life like a dash.

Many besides Kant have recognized the power of such reasoning. The poet Percy Shelley asked, "Have we existed before birth? . . . Does [this soul, or "principle"] see, hear, feel, before its combination with those organs on which sensation depends? Does it reason, imagine, apprehend, without those ideas which sensation alone can communicate?" He then concludes with simple logic: "If we have not existed before birth; . . . then there are no grounds for supposition that we shall continue to exist after our existence has apparently ceased." Even the arch-skeptic David Hume found that argument appealing, holding that nature itself teaches us that "*what is incorruptible must also be ingenerable* [incapable of being created]. The soul, therefore, if immortal, existed before our birth." The great Jewish rabbi Menasseh ben Israel thought premortal existence even *more* reasonable than postmortal existence, but certainly one had to imply the other. More recently, the philosopher Bertrand Russell questioned "whether it was reasonable to suppose that something immortal could just suddenly begin in time."

A pressing problem, of course, is why would we not remember more fully our existence before birth? (Nothing strange in that, mused Tennyson, "For is not our first year forgot?"). Early Christians thought it likely that forgetting was a tender mercy, as did Alexander Pope. We may be uneasy on earth, remote and "confined" from our true "home"; but if our vision were not limited to our "present state . . . who could [endure] being here below?" As a contemporary stated more simply, "We had been inexpressibly more miserable, if we had retained the memory of our former Glory, and past Actions."

The veil of forgetfulness that divides eternity in two has its own powerful justifications. Philip Barlow, a modern religious scholar, has written eloquently of the surprising value of the veil:

> My impression is that, informed and animated by a thoughtful faith in a wider horizon, the veil quite properly funnels the bulk of our attention to the here and now: on the time, people, problems, and opportunities of this day, this moment. Despite glimpses of eternal purposes that come as gifts and hopes, my life unfolds in tremendous, all-but-complete ignorance of our mysterious universe. There is no proving God to others. Ultimate reality is not something we know; it is something in which we put our trust. . . . The veil is not a curse or cause for existential lament. It is necessary to our stage of progression as beings. While we search, listen, and pray for comfort and direction beyond our sphere, the veil—the necessary epistemic distance from this "beyond"—affords us freedom for independent action not possible if we could literally and readily see God smiling or frowning at each move. And freedom independently to discern and choose between good and evil (morality) and good and bad (quality) is at the core of our purpose, as the powerful mythos of Genesis suggests.

The greatest virtue of the idea of premortal existence, undoubtedly, is in its solution to the problem of human freedom more generally. If our life carries hidden within its core our own eternal past, then we are free in a way no alternate conception of human existence can account for. Philosophers and theologians have debated endlessly the problem of reconciling moral freedom with divine foreknowledge. How can we freely choose, if God knows unerringly what we will choose? But that problem of free will pales beside the more daunting challenge of how we can freely choose, if God made us—body and soul, mind and will, genes and instincts, predispositions and predilections, tastes and desires?

One can say, God created us and He created us free. But that just substitutes a declaration for an explanation. No, if God is the sole author of all that is, then we cannot find our way clear to believe He is not responsible for our choices. The ancients knew that something is free only if it is not caused or created by something else, and a twentieth-century philosopher wrote with stark simplicity: If God created our souls, He "could have prevented all sin by creating us with better natures and in more favorable surroundings. . . . Hence we should not be responsible for our sins to God."

That is the same logic by which we assign blame in all other instances where there is a creator and a thing created. If a bridge collapses, we hold responsible the person who designed the bridge or executed its construction. If a computer program misperforms an operation, we know a programmer or data entry person was at fault. When the *Challenger* explodes or a buffet dinner leads to a salmonella outbreak, we know somewhere someone failed. If we properly rear offspring who then choose to lie or steal, we are only exonerated because no one would imagine us to be the creators of the spirit that animates and informs their being. We generally choose between imputing the design of their bodies and minds to evolutionary and biological processes, in which case we are off the hook. Or we impute the creation of their essential being to God, in which case it would seem He, and no one else, deserves blame.

But the fact is, as adults with moral awareness, we sense *we* are responsible for our own choices. And the reason we know we are is because we feel guilt when we do something wrong. We are not speaking here of the oppressive, destructive self-loathing or self-hatred that masquerades as conscience; by guilt we mean the inward call to be truer to our better selves. Legitimate guilt is to the spirit what the sharp protest of a twisted ankle is to the foot: its purpose is to hurt enough to stop you from crippling yourself further. Its function is to *prevent* more pain, not expand it. This kind of guilt comes from the light and beckons us to follow; its counterfeit takes us only deeper into the darkness of despair. For, as William Law wrote, "Christ never was, nor can be, in any creature but purely as a spirit of love."

The modern era has given us a dozen reasons to explain away those legitimate feelings of guilt we all experience. We can call these feelings the product of social conditioning or fear of a father figure. We can resort to the notion of a Freudian superego or a Nietzschean self-directed will to power. We can, more commonly, attribute guilt to simple religious indoctrination, but no rationalization can allay the insistent knowledge that we all confess in moments of secret honesty: we do wrong because we make a decision to do so, and we feel guilty because we know we could have acted differently. That means we know we had other options than the one we chose. If we could have acted differently, then we were free to act differently at that moment of choice. Guilt, the legitimate remorse we feel for a deliberate decision to do wrong, is all the proof we need that arguments about determinism and predestination are a philosopher's game. Guilt is how we know we are free to choose.

Nothing else we can say about our identity is as certain or fundamental. We are not born good or evil. We are born free. We may feel the prick of conscience, the demands of duty, the weight of heredity, all guiding us through—or onto—the shoals of life. Still, we are free to regard our circumstances, and to respond to our predicament, in accordance with a set of desires we have the power to school and shape. Our lives are more like a canvas on which we paint, than a script we need to learn—though the illusion of the latter appeals to us by its lower risk. It is easier to learn a part than create a work of art. The mystery is, how can I be free to shape my own desires, how can I be responsible for the inclinations of my heart, for my tendency to love light or darkness, if God created my spirit out of nothing, calling me into existence by His sovereign power, only at the moment of my birth or conception?

One of the great modern philosophers of human freedom, Jean-Paul Sartre, like most Existentialist philosophers, rejected God on this very basis. He realized that authentic freedom required self-creation. We must be free to make our own choices, if we are to create a genuine identity of authenticity and dignity. And that freedom is simply incompatible with our existence as products, beings whose origin, constitution, and will, are created by Another. Of course, if we throw out God, as Sartre does, we still have our genes, our environment, our "too, too solid flesh," and so much else to contend with. We cannot simply step outside the causal links of the chain that led to us, and pretend we created ourselves unhindered and untouched by the cumbersome baggage of the species and of the family name we inherited at birth.

No, we may remove God, but we cannot remove our past and present circumstances. With or without God, regardless of Sartre's dream of independence, we are left with the same problem. In our present, earthly form, we are clearly the product of forces outside our control that influence our personality, inform our character, and shape our wants and desires. And yet, we know we are free. How can this be, unless there is something at the heart of our identity that was *not* shaped by environment, *not* inherited from our parents, and *not* even created by God? This dilemma has one reasonable resolution, as the Cambridge philosopher John Wisdom summarized: "However far back we go," only belief in pre-existence can reconcile the principle of free will and the recognition that every event has a cause.

Some scholars who thought deeply about the nature of sin came to the same conclusion that only preexistence can explain human freedom. It is no solution simply to insist that God made us free. Sin must mean accountability, reasoned the German theologian Julius Müller. Accountability must mean the freedom to choose. And human freedom can only have its roots "in a sphere beyond the range of time, wherein alone pure and unconditioned self-determination is possible. In this region we must seek that power of original choice." Müller concluded, as did McTaggart and Wisdom, that the only basis for human freedom and human accountability is a human soul that existed before birth as it will after death. Moral freedom demands preexistence, and preexistence explains human freedom.

The validity of this argument was recognized by one of Wisdom's fellow philosophers, Helen Smith, who agreed the two concepts were powerfully linked. However, she found the idea of preexistence so unpalatable that she wrote she would prefer to abandon her belief in human accountability, than accept the only foundation for human accountability, i.e., a preexistent human soul. She would rather give up the ideas of guilt and moral responsibility, in other words, than accept a soul with an eternal past. But for those who consider the call of conscience and personal responsibility to be gifts rather than inconveniences, embracing an eternal past seems a more reasonable choice. M. F. Burnyeat, a Fellow of the British Academy, noted in this regard that "however many readers . . . believe that their soul will survive death, rather few, I imagine, believe that it also pre-existed their birth. The religions that have shaped Western culture are so inhospitable to the idea of pre-existence that you probably reject the thought out of hand, for no good reason."

That takes us back to seventeenth-century Henry More, who was convinced that "All Intellectual Spirits that ever were, are, or ever shall be, sprung up with the Light, . . . infinite Myriads of Free

Agents which were the Framers of their own Fortunes." If the spark of human consciousness is eternal and undetermined, then God did not predispose us in any direction, set our course toward the evil or the good. Our original choice, or one of them, judging by our present state and possibilities, must have been a response to a set of options given us by a superior Being, which led to our presence in the world (since we quite clearly didn't get here on our own, and if we were simply cast adrift on the shore of this strange world, where is the freedom in that?).

A text attributed to Abraham, found in the Pearl of Great Price, describes just such a primordial drama in which assembled hosts collectively assented to a proposal that would transition them from their "first estate," a dwelling in a pre-earthly realm, to a "second estate," or our current mortal realm.

> Now the Lord had shown unto me, Abraham, the intelligences that were organized before the world was; . . . ; And God saw these souls that they were good, . . . and he said unto me: Abraham, thou art one of them; thou wast chosen before thou wast born. And there stood one among them that was like unto God, and He said unto those who were with him: We will go down, for there is space there, and we will take of these materials, and we will make an earth whereon these may dwell; . . . and they who keep their second estate shall have glory added upon their heads for ever and ever.

The beauty of this conception is twofold: first, it suggests that birth into this world represents a step forward in an eternal process of development and growth, not a descent or regression from a primal goodness. God's work is therefore first and foremost educative and constructive, not reparative. Life is pain but it is not punishment, and it begins in a season of hope—for all of us, not just our mythic parents.

Second, co-participation in the decision to embark on a mortal sojourn does not eliminate the problem of evil, but it dramatically alters it. If we were involved in the deliberations that culminated in creating and peopling this world, then we are not passive victims of providence. We would have entered into the conditions of this mortal state aware of the harrowing hazards mortality entails.

Such co-participation does not mitigate the horror of what many experience in this life. The enormity of evil may still appall and confound us. God's failure to intervene may distress and alienate us. Our personal experience of loss and loneliness may overwhelm us. But the suspicion that we were party to the terms of our own predicament may give heart when no other solace is to be found.

Another startling insight emerges from the paradigm of preexistence. If it is true that "Man was also in the beginning with God," that "Intelligence, or the light of truth, was not created or made, neither indeed can be," then we have an eternal past. And if we have an eternal past, then humans—like God—inhabit a universe that has always existed. The implications of this view are nothing short of shattering, fraught with possibilities that are simultaneously heady and humbling. It would suggest the possibility that "God, angels and men are all of one species." Our ancestry and potential are rooted in a divine pattern.

Soberingly, if we are co-eternal with God, then it is not God's creation of the human out of nothing that defines our essential relationship to Him. It is His freely made choice to inaugurate and sustain loving relationships, and our choice to reciprocate, that are at the core of our relationship to the Divine. "We love Him because He first loved us." It means that deep in the primeval past, before the earth was formed or the first man or woman created, grace irrupted into the universe. Before Adam tilled the earth or Eve bore her first child, God had already set His heart upon the race of men, and designed to bring them into His own heavenly sphere.

He is our Father, insofar as He chose to father us. In some fashion, beyond our present reckoning or strength to imagine, God deigned to take us in our undeveloped, unformed, embryonic state, and shepherd us in the direction of a more abundant life. He is our Creator, insofar as He organized the stars and the earth and inaugurated those processes by which we have our present shape and form. In this version of a primordial drama, described by Joseph Smith, God looks upon a vast multitude of unembodied intelligences, has compassion on their relative weakness and vulnerability, and "agrees to form them tabernacles." Our profoundly felt frailty and dependence dispel any illusion that co-eternity means co-equality. Our perennial longing for Home affirms a relationship rooted in the love of a child for a tender parent, not in the obsequiousness of a vassal toward his lord, or of a courtier toward his king, though He is both our Lord and King.

CHAPTER THREE

We Are That We Might Have Joy

Mortality is an ascent, not a fall, and we carry infinite potential into a world of sin and sorrow.

"Sin is behovely [necessary and beneficial], but all shall be well, and all shall be well, and all manner of things shall be well."

The angel hosts with freshness go,
And seek with laughter what to brave;—
. . . And from a cliff-top is proclaimed
The gathering of the souls for birth,
The trial by existence named,
The obscuration upon earth. . . .
And the more loitering are turned
To view once more the sacrifice
Of those who for some good discerned
Will gladly give up paradise.

So did Robert Frost, the great American poet, imagine the scene in heaven as multitudes of spirits prepared to descend, or perhaps, given the opportunities in store, to *ascend* to earth. A hundred years earlier, another poet doubted the loss of paradise was either desirable or fair. In Lord Byron's play about the aftermath of Adam's and Eve's exile from Eden, an angry Cain finds himself in a world of pain and death. "I was unborn: I sought not to be born," he complains. Thus, two different scenarios offer themselves to our choosing. In this Byronic version, we are—like Cain—helpless victims of decisions made by someone else. The Fall was a catastrophe—a catastrophe Christ would mitigate, but a catastrophe nonetheless. For centuries, the Adamic decision to defy the gentle command of a generous God was viewed as such an infinite betrayal that the universe itself could not contain it; the repercussions of Eve's primeval gesture overflows into generations millennia removed, children and children's children yet unborn. The Original Sin has seemed to millions to be a choice of such unforgivable pride in the face of such infinite goodness that the penalty should descend not just upon the first couple, but upon their descendants forever.

That is why Byron's Cain rebels against paying for a choice he had no part in making, deprived of paradise through no fault of his own. To Cain, we are all pawns in a game of the gods and now all of human history unfolds as a bleak aftermath to a cosmic catastrophe. True enough, this version of life's meaning assigns the role of savior to the Son of God, and all may yet end in consoling splendor. But in this story of Original Sin, redemption and salvation emphasize our "lostness." Our damnation or alienation is a natural, default condition from which we need rescue. The implications of this scenario are immense. Western culture has been largely shaped by this narrative that depicts our mythic ancestors as cosmic failures and betrayers of their race, and ourselves as inmates of an earthly prison to which we are sentenced before we are born.

Or, we might conceive a narrative more like Frost's—one in which we willingly gave up paradise for what the poet called a greater "good discerned." The question is, what greater good can life entail? Why leave heaven for a vale of tears? The text of Genesis gives us some clues. Eve's and Adam's decision to eat the fruit of the tree, and thus forsake their paradise, may be an allegory for—or perhaps a counterpart to—our own decision to accept the conditions of mortality, in exchange for a heavenly paradise.

We should notice that in the story of the Garden, Adam and Eve are presented with options that are more complex than the simple Right and Wrong of Sunday sermons. Certainly a prohibition is violated, and in that sense there is a transgression. But, as the philosopher Hegel argued forcefully, the most tragic predicaments in which we find ourselves are those that require a choice between competing Goods, *not* Good and Evil. The author of Genesis frames Eve's choice as just such a dilemma, a choice between the safety and security of the Garden, and the goodness, beauty, and wisdom that come at the price—and only at the price—of painful lived experience. Her decision is more worthy of admiration for its courage and initiative, than reproach for its rebellion. This is apparent for a number of reasons.

First, the tree *was*, according to the author, *good* for food, a *delight to the eyes*, and desirable to make one *wise*. And those motives, not rebelliousness or perverseness, are what the author of Genesis specifically attributes to Eve as she makes her choice. She is not tempted by a frivolous curiosity or hunger for power. She is not facilely manipulated or co-opted to a nefarious scheme. She is depicted as a woman in pursuit of the Good, the True, the Beautiful.

Second, Adam and Eve are obviously represented as already having some knowledge of good and evil, or they could hardly be accountable for their decision. If, before eating the fruit they are without any moral discernment whatever, it makes no sense to call that act a sin. The implication is that they were already possessed of some knowledge of good and evil, *in theory*. The knowledge of good and evil which they lacked is *experiential* knowledge. Eve's rationale for eating the fruit emphasizes a kind of knowledge that is acquired bodily, empirically. Eve is drawn to a fruit that is good to the *taste*, a delight to *the eyes*. The wisdom to which she aspires is acquired through experiential immersion. In fact, "knowledge" as used biblically generally has this connotation of a knowledge that is personal, relational, intimate—rather than abstract, cerebral, or theoretical. (As when Adam "knew" his wife and she conceived.) As events prove, the Tree of Knowledge serves as a gateway to the whole gamut of lived experience, the sweaty toil of labor, the bodily agony of childbirth, as well as physical susceptibility to decay and death.

Third, in consequence of Eve's choice, God does three significant things: He notes they have now become "as one of us," indicating some kind of growth has been initiated. He curses the ground "for [their] sake or "on [their] account," suggesting He is facilitating rather than punishing their decision to encounter a world of trial and opposites. And He does not forbid them immortality, but defers their immortality for a period. He prevents them from eating of the Tree of Life, since that would cause them to "live forever," before the period of testing and growth had accomplished its perfecting work. *After* this mortal stage of growth is complete, as we see in the vision of the Revelator, the righteous reenter a celestial paradise with not one, but twelve Trees of Life.

These events suggest something more in the nature of an unfolding plan, than a God's frantic damage control. They also suggest why it is reasonable to read the story of the Garden as representing a set of competing, difficult options. Adam and Eve may avoid the tree, and continue to dwell in God's presence. Or, they may partake of the fruit and experience temporary exile, death, and pain—along with the transcendent possibility of a future hardly to be fathomed ("you shall be as the gods"). The decision is theirs. A nineteenth-century recasting of the scripture reads, "Thou mayest choose for thyself, for it is given unto thee." There is a hint, in other words, that the prohibition was more in the nature of a warning, articulating the costly consequences of disregarding the restriction. And so they do choose for themselves.

At Eve's courageous instigation, they opt to lose paradise, hoping to eventually regain heaven—but transformed and ennobled by the schoolhouse of experience that comprises mortality. Mortality, therefore, immersion in bodily, earthly experience, is vital to becoming like God. In this version of the story, we find ourselves in the same dreary world. But the debris of the first transgression—pain and death especially—is a dark and difficult middle passage, not the origin, in our spiritual odyssey. Ascent into mortality is a precursor to something even greater than the paradise we left. As a Book of Mormon scripture summarizes, "Adam [and Eve] fell that men might be; and men are, that they might have joy."

This is not the traditional reading of Genesis, the fall of Adam, or the meaning of mortality. But it is a version that has had its advocates. In the first Christian centuries, commentators found Adam and Eve's departure from the Garden and God's act of clothing them with skins to be a clear metaphor for their descent into a world, where God clothed their souls in earthly bodies. The medieval mystic Julian of Norwich wrote in response to a vision in which she saw the "Lorde" send his servant Man to dwell on earth. The servant, representing Adam, "runs in great haste for love to do his Lorde's will," but soon stumbles and falls. Julian attended carefully to see what blame or retribution should befall the servant. To her surprise, "verily there was none seen, for only his good will and his great desire was the cause of his falling."

In fact, the Lord explains that, since Adam undertook his task out of love and "good wylle," he deserves by right to be compensated for his pain and suffering, his fear and anxiety, to an extent "above that he would have known if he had not fallen." In fact, she continues, not only Adam, but "alle manne" [all men] are so seen by God. In "falling," in other words, Adam and Eve and their posterity, agreed to temporarily abandon a noble heritage and dwelling with

God himself. They deserve in consequence a compensation as rich or richer than the goodly state and condition they risked in going forth.

In the Jewish tradition, renowned seventeenth-century rabbi Menasseh ben Israel held that human souls existed before embodiment, not just as ideas in the mind of God, but as entities with whom He actually consulted before Creation, in order to make sure He did not clothe them with matter against their will. Kabbalists such as Moses de León agreed that birth is ascent, not fall, and life's purpose is educative, not punitive. "The purpose of the human soul entering this body is to display her powers and actions in this world, for she needs an instrument. . . . Thereby she perfects herself above and below, attaining a higher state by being fulfilled in all her dimensions. . . . At first, before descending to this world, the soul is imperfect; she is lacking something. By descending to this world, she is perfected in every dimension."

But how perfected, how completed? What does separation from God, immersion in the crucible of life, and the attainment of the body, gain the spirit? The ancient philosopher Plato, just as those figures above, thought life was most likely a choice—even the circumstances of our birth and lot in life. He described a scenario in which spirits were allowed to select their lives from a range of situations and environments. Intuitively, most would choose the easy and attractive path through mortality, but Plato indicates that—contrary to expectations—the comfortable, effortless life was, in all likelihood, not the life most wisely chosen. The greater good mortality offered us, in Plato's view, was the quest for greater virtue and goodness. In that light, "call a life worse," he said, "if it leads a soul to become more unjust, and better if it leads the soul to become more just."

We have no way of knowing, of course, why some are born in health and affluence, while others enter broken bodies or broken homes, or emerge into a realm of war or hunger. So we cannot give definite meaning to our place in the world, or to our neighbor's. But Plato's reflections should give us pause and invite both humility and hope. Humility, because if we chose our lot in life, there is every reason to suspect merit, and not disfavor, is behind disadvantaged birth. A blighted life may have been the more courageous choice—at least it was for Plato. Though the first act of the play was obscure, its hidden details make any judgments in this second act so much foolish speculation. So how can we feel pride in our own blessedness, or condescension at another's misfortune? And Plato's reflections should give us hope, because his myth reminds us that suffering can be sanctifying, that pain is not punishment, and that the path to virtue is fraught with opposition.

All of which goes to explain why Darwin had much to teach us, not just about physical evolution, but about spiritual evolution as well. This is especially true in his account of the honeybee, which well serves as a parable for our ascent into mortal life. The honeybee, Darwin points out in his *Origin of Species*, has a glaring defect as a creature. Its poison is effective in killing prey, enabling it to defend itself and its nest. But delivery of that poison can only come at the cost of its own life. Darwin speculates that this is because the bee's stinger was originally "a boring and serrated instrument," probably used for extracting food from fibrous sources. It was therefore, in his words, "not perfected for its present purpose" of defense.

The question, of course, is why has the stinger not evolved into something more perfect in the millions of years since? Why did the evolutionary process cease? Why did natural selection not accomplish its end of making the bee as perfect as possible? Certainly, a bee that can kill without sacrificing its life is an improvement over one that cannot. A simple smoothing of the bee's serrated edge would do the trick quite nicely and efficiently. Why was the bee's progress toward species perfection aborted so precipitously and—in the case of myriad individuals and even hives—calamitously?

This is Darwin's explanation: "Natural selection tends only to make each organic being as perfect as, or slightly more perfect than, the other inhabitants of the same country with which it comes into competition. And we see that this is the standard of perfection attained under nature." And then he adds this declaration: "Natural selection will not produce absolute perfection." What he means is this: the law of natural selection, what Herbert Spencer will call the principle of survival of the fittest, ensures that any competition for limited resources will favor those who are in any way advantaged over their competitors. It will weed out those who are inferior or even mediocre, and allow to prevail those who have greater strength, agility, speed, or survival skills.

The long-term effect of this principle is to breed creatures that are, in Darwin's terms, "more perfect than their peers." But the law of natural selection also has a striking limitation, and this is what he means by saying it can never produce absolute perfection. This limitation is perfectly illustrated by the common honeybee. In the struggle for survival, the bee's development, even with a flawed stinger, was sufficient to securely establish its position in the natural world. Once it achieved species equilibrium, and lacking conflict and opposition to further challenge, stimulate, and refine its development, its progress was essentially halted. As William Blake said, in one of the greatest insights of the modern age, "without contraries, is no progression." We are apparently made of the same stuff as Darwin's honeybee. We need the continuing spiritual friction of difficulty, opposition, and hardship, or we will suffer the same stasis as the bee.

In this context, one can understand why instead of deploring Eve's and Adam's transgression, one might find in it a cause for rejoicing. If we take seriously God's words that the couple "has become like one of us," then human history does indeed take a new direction here. In some incontrovertible sense this new direction is an ascent, and not a fall. Paradise is lost, but divinity appears on the distant horizon. In one version of the aftermath, Adam and Eve give momentous new meaning to the term, "Fortunate Fall": "And in that day Adam blessed God, and was filled, and began to prophesy concerning all the families of the earth, saying: Blessed be the name of God, for because of my transgression my eyes are opened, and in this life I shall have joy, and again in the flesh I shall see God. And Eve, his wife, heard all these things and was glad, saying: Were it not for our transgression we . . . never should have known good and evil."

If our birth is a choice and not a cosmic quirk, if life represents the opportunity for further progress in acquiring the virtue and holiness that characterize God, and if sin is the educative consequence of bad choices, then Fall and Damnation are not the best terms to describe the human predicament. And guilt, original or otherwise, is not the central human problem. Inadequacy, insufficiency, weakness, and spiritual immaturity, are more accurate descriptors of a soul in the early stages of heavenly development. Krister Stendahl, Lutheran Bishop of Stockholm and dean of the Harvard Divinity School, lamented the early historical turn that took Christianity in the direction of more negative characterizations and preoccupations. And he blames it on a misreading of Paul the Apostle:

> The point where Paul's experience intersects with his . . . understanding of the faith, furthermore, is not "sin" with its correlate "forgiveness." It is rather when Paul speaks about his weakness that we feel his deeply personal pain. Once more we find something surprisingly different from the Christian language that most of us take for granted: it seems that Paul never felt guilt in the face of this weakness—pain, yes, but not guilt. It is not in the drama of the saving of Paul the sinner, but it is in the drama of Paul's coming to grips with what he calls his "weakness" that we find the most experiential level of Paul's theology.

Christianity's fixation on the "plagued conscience" is a development Stendahl traces to Augustine three centuries after Paul, and then to the Reformers over a thousand years later. Sinfulness and guilt assumed thereafter center stage in the Christian drama. For most of Christian history, all humans were considered to share in a guilt and a depravity traceable to our biblical parents. "In Adam's Fall, We sinned all," as the New England primer taught generations of schoolchildren. Such guilt was said to attach to us from our birth, prior to and independently of individual choice. And at the same time, the doctrine of Original Sin asserted a universal predisposition in human nature toward evil rather than good.

A look at any of today's headlines seems to bear out a general tendency toward evil in human nature. As the joke has it, Original Sin is the only empirically verifiable doctrine of the Christian faith. It is not just a case that a significant segment of the population seems to have gone over to the dark side, but that in each and every one of us, even those striving to do good, we recognize the allure of evil. So the narrative that develops is of a universal condemnation. The entire human race is lost, fallen, damned, waiting and hoping for rescue, for salvation.

Surely this is a perverse vision and a slander upon God. It suggests His plan was derailed before it got off the ground, that He is a brilliant repairman but a poor designer. God's creation of the human race begins in catastrophe and is in need of salvaging. That we should be condemned, punished, accounted guilty, for crimes of our ancestors, is a concept repugnant to every conception of human justice. What knowledge of Good and Evil did we acquire, that does not forewarn us against such twistings of moral logic? What could be more debilitating than to begin life with a premise of debasement rather than blessedness, to see our birth as an inherited perdition rather than the gift of opportunity, to imagine our origins as steeped in sin rather than trailing clouds of glory?

No wonder Harriet Beecher Stowe's brother, the preacher Edward Beecher, believed that "if there is in fact a malignant spirit, of great and all-pervading power, intent on making a fixed and steady opposition to the progress of the cause of God," he would "pervert and disgrace" the story of our true origins in a premortal world, and our true relation to God. "He would present it in false and odious combinations. . . . He would fill the church and ministry with a prejudgment against it."

At the cost of his own promising career in the ministry, Beecher labored to restore to Christianity the doctrine of human spirits, living "in a previous state of existence," free-agents with the power of choice and self-determination "as the laws of honor and right demanded." As a consequence, he wrote, we find ourselves here not as sick souls who inherited another's illness, not as inmates condemned for another's crime, but as students embarked on the imitation of the Divine. "Life, from beginning to end, [is] a constant system of education for eternity."

How different the outlook if the divine plan were originally about elevation rather than remedy, advancement rather than repair. Without question, we have entered upon a world where barriers of every sort conspire to alienate us further from God and our heavenly home. Our condition in the world is one of estrangement, and obliviousness. We erect false idols to replace the God we have forgotten, and we rapidly and readily adapt to ambitions and appetites shaped more by our biology than our true ancestry. As branches cut off from the true vine that is God, we are indeed at risk of being overwhelmed by temptation, engulfed in sin.

In his play *The War in Heaven*, Sam Shepard captures the sense of shock and dislocation felt by a spirit so abruptly thrown into a world that is fallen in all those ways:

> *I died*
> *the day I was born*
> . . .
> *I am here*
> *by mistake*
> *I'm not sure how it happened*

I crashed
I know I crashed
in these streets
I came down
I don't know what went wrong
I was a part of something
I remember being
a member
I was moving
I had certain orders
a mission.

The spirit of the poem is haunted by intimations of something "ancient old old old before birth even." Just as Shepard's unsettled spirit, we find a dissonance between the creature of nature and one that longs for home. We often feel, as Goethe's Faust does, that

Two souls, alas, are dwelling in my breast,
And either would be severed from its brother;
The one holds fast with joyous earthy lust
Onto the world of man with organs clinging;
The other soars impassioned from the dust,
To realms of lofty forebears winging.

Sin is real, and the barriers it erects between us and other beings—both human and divine—is its most pernicious consequence. That is the collateral damage incident to the necessary trial and testing and growth of mortality. Sin has its part to play, but it is neither our original condition, nor our inherent nature. Immanuel Kant, the greatest philosopher of the eighteenth century, believed "there is one thing in our soul which we cannot cease from regarding with the highest wonder . . . and that is the original moral predisposition itself in us." Why, he continues, do we find ourselves consumed by the demands of our physical nature, and yet feel so "unworthy of existence, if we cater to their satisfaction"? It is not an inherited depravity, but "a divine origin" that this deepest nature reveals, and that insight "acts . . . upon the spirit even to the point of exaltation." If we only live to satisfy our physical desires, we are suffocating our spiritual selves.

Poets, as well, have rebelled against an uncompromisingly dour view of human nature, finding it simply didn't resonate with their own experience of infancy and youth especially. Thomas Traherne, for instance, poetically recalled the transition from heaven to earth life as one of exciting possibility rather than prison or purgatory.

> *Long time before I in my mother's womb was born,*
> *A God preparing did this glorious store,*
> *The world, for me adorn.*
> *Into this Eden so divine and fair,*
> *So wide and bright, I come His son and heir.*
> *A stranger here.*

In another poem, he again rejects the mythology of a universal fall:

> *How like an angel came I down!*
> *How bright are all things here!*
> *When first among His works I did appear*
> *Oh, how their glory me did crown!*
> *The world resembled His eternity,*
> *In which my soul did walk.*

It is not the idea of sin that Traherne rejects. Coming from a prior state of innocence, we are at the beginning of our mortal life in the same position as Eve and Adam: free to choose and shape our own nature. Writing in the seventeenth century, he can only marvel at how his memories put him outside the more generally accepted version of our degenerate place and standing in the world.

But that which most I wonder at, which most
I did esteem my bliss, which most I boast
And ever shall enjoy, is that within
I felt no stain nor spot of sin.
No darkness then did overshade,
But all within was pure and bright,
No guilt did crush nor fear invade,
But all my soul was full of light.
A joyful sense and purity
Is all I can remember. . . .
I was an Adam there,
A little Adam in a sphere
Of joys! . . .

Like Adam, we find sin enough. But we find it on our own, without having to borrow any from our first parents. How then are we to understand the fact that we come to earth, as Traherne wrote, "full of light," but soon find ourselves to be weak and selfish, often carnal and worldly, and frequently malicious instruments of our own and others' harm. This nature seems most reasonably understood as an imperfect, upwardly striving soul, enmeshed in a material body with all the hormones, instincts, appetites, propensities, and cravings that a vessel encompassed in flesh is heir to.

We do not need an ancestral scapegoat or a theology of inherited sin to understand what any student of human biology does. Our DNA programs us to look out for our own survival, to make sex and food our priorities, and to respond to threats to our security or well-being with suspicion, hostility, or aggression. Even the religious recognize that the body is of the earth and subject to the conditions of the material world. That condition, however, is not our punishment, it is our challenge. "Why came ye to this world of woe?" asked Mormon apostle Parley Pratt. "You came to the earth to be born of flesh, / To fashion and perfect your earthly house."

The very burden of our corporeal humanity, with all its natural, selfish, and passion-driven attributes, apparently serves the divine purpose behind embodiment. Our challenge is to ennoble and improve the fractious and frequently uncooperative body we inherit at birth. However, the body is not just our little kingdom, our private domain to discipline, subject, and perfect. It is a glorious end in itself.

Central to all Christian conceptions of human aspiration is the idea of the *imitatio Christi*, the imitation of Christ, the elevation of Christ as the supreme example we attempt to emulate. Some writers saw Christ's acquisition of a mortal body to be a process that all premortal souls followed. For this reason, one sixteenth-century biblical scholar called human birth "a little Incarnation." Christ did not abandon His body after His death, but took it up again in a glorified state, and with it ascended to heaven, with a promise to return in like fashion.

We might, therefore, reasonably hypothesize that Christ saw His own incarnation as progression, rather than regression. He knew only the body and soul, "inseparably connected, receive a fullness of joy." Some early church fathers saw His incarnation as ennobling the body, rather than degrading the Divine. Gregory Nazianzen wrote of a day in Christ's mortal life, "Perhaps He goes to sleep, in order that He may bless sleep . . . ; perhaps He is tired that He may hallow weariness also; perhaps He weeps that He may make tears blessed."

As the resurrected Christ assumed a perfected and glorified body before ascending to heaven, so might we envision our own mortality in terms of a body which enhances, rather than hinders, our spiritual progression. Certainly, it makes more sense to see the bodily senses as portals of joy, than as dangerous distractions. There are those who, like a Greek philosopher, set out to attain the lofty realms of pure thought, or to lose themselves in a life of pure contemplation, remote from the world of the body, with its earthy limitations. But why would one want to do so? We think through the mind, but we live through the body. God's universe reflects the beauty and variety of a matchless artist, who delights in color and music and texture and fragrance—and the five senses are our windows onto this world of sight and sound and taste. How can we not rejoice with the poet Gerard Manley Hopkins, that "the world is charged with the glory of God; it will flame out, like shining from shook foil"? How can we not feel to exclaim with him,

Glory be to God for dappled things
For skies of couple-colour as a brinded cow;
For rose-moles all in stipple upon trout that swim;
Fresh-firecoal chestnut-falls; finches' wings;
Landscapes plotted and pieced—fold, fallow, and plough;
And all trades, their gear and tackle and trim.

All things counter, original, spare, strange;
Whatever is fickle, freckled (who knows how?)
With swift, slow; sweet, sour; adazzle, dim;
He fathers-forth whose beauty is past change:
Praise Him.

If the book of nature is written in the language of God, the message seems to be, as Brigham Young states, "There is no enjoyment, no comfort, no pleasure, nothing that the human heart can imagine . . . that tends to beautify, happify, make comfortable and peaceful, and exalt the feelings of mortals, but what the Lord has in store for His people." For those inclined to make worldly pleasures their principal pursuit, dangers, of course, lurk. All feasting may become gluttony. But that is not to say the food was not delicious and designed to satisfy.

The philosopher Bertrand Russell may have stopped short of seeing the giver behind the gift, but he was right about the poverty of puritanism for its own sake. "The secret of happiness is this: let your interests be as wide as possible," he said. He then made his point with the simple example of a taste for strawberries. "There is no abstract and impersonal proof either that strawberries are good or that they are not good. To the man who likes them they are good, to the man who dislikes them they are not. But the man who likes them has a pleasure which the other does not have; to that extent his life is more enjoyable and he is better adapted to the world in which both must live. . . . The more things a man is interested in, the more opportunities of happiness he has."

Might an increased capacity for happiness in fact be the ultimate goal of human life, the "object and design of our existence"? If so, children seem an instructive example of what the preconditions of happiness might be, at least when it comes to the delights of bodily existence. The sheer exuberance children express as they engage the world, their reveling in the simple delights of childhood, their openness to their world, is the envy of every adult.

Arriving late to drop off our four-year-old at a friend's house, we watched her race for the front door like a shot, desperate to recoup lost time. Suddenly her legs stopped stiffly, and she skidded to a halt. Assuming she had forgotten something, we expected her to return, but she only backed up several hurried steps. She then bent sharply at the waist until her nose almost touched the ground and rested it on a solitary flower along the walkway. With arms akimbo, she slowly inhaled with her whole body, then, satisfied she had consumed the flower's entire fragrance, streaked back onto the porch and through the door. Children illustrate the truth that "the great principle of happiness consists in having a body." As Wordsworth noted, "To that dreamlike vividness and splendor which invest objects of sight in childhood, every one, I believe, if he would look back, could bear testimony."

Children are at the beginning of their mortal trials, and their spirits as yet uncalloused. Perfection implies conquest of trial and temptation, not immunity from them, which is why John Milton said he could not "praise a fugitive and cloistered Vertue unexercised and unbreath'd." Still, the spontaneity, the honesty, the guilelessness and generous affection of children is a type of perfection, if not its fullness, and suggests a larger truth: that "the nearer man approaches perfection, the clearer are his views, and the greater are his enjoyments." Our task, it would seem, is to retain or recapture the innocence with which we began this life, while passing through the crucible we call mortality.

We therefore should not see the body and spirit in opposition. The fact that Christ chose children as a model for moral goodness means socialization, not incarnation, is the source of our ills. When Paul condemned the "natural man," he specifically associated it with an *acquired,* not an *innate* worldliness. "Human wisdom" and "the spirit of the world" are its hallmarks, he said, not the senses and passions. Our task is to school our appetites, not suppress them, to make them work in concert with a will that disciplines the spirit as much as the flesh. For desire has both spiritual and bodily expression, and our life is a journey to purify both. Along the way, we discipline and honor the body, even as we aspire to perfect the soul, finding in the end that the body and spirit, fitly framed together, do indeed provide the deepest joy.

We find that life is labor, a stage in a journey where we feel the draw of a familiar goal, where a sense of a "divine origin, acts . . . upon the spirit." An ancient allegory, "The Hymn of the Pearl," recorded in a book of scripture never canonized, gives expression to the purpose of this life, traceable to a premortal past, not a random birth in recent time. The first stanza tells of royal parents who send their son on a quest in search of a great pearl. His parents bless him, clothe him, and send him on his way:

> *When I was a little child living*
> *in my father's palace in his kingdom,*
> *happy in the glories and riches*
> *of my family that nurtured me,*

my parents gave me supplies
and sent me on a mission
from our home in the east. . . .
They took off my bright robe of glory,
which they had made for me out of love,
and took away my purple toga,
which was woven to fit my stature.
They made a covenant with me
and wrote it in my heart so I would not forget:
"When you go down into Egypt
and bring back the one pearl
that lies in the middle of the sea
and is guarded by the snorting serpent,
you will again put on your robe of glory
and your toga over it,
and with your brother, our next in rank,
you will be heir in our kingdom."

In this new realm, he is soon distracted from his mission. Once among the many strangers, he recalls, "I put on a robe like theirs" and

fell into a deep sleep.
I forgot that I was a son of kings
and served their king.
I forgot the pearl
for which my parents had sent me.

His alarmed parents, together with his crown prince brother, send him a letter reminding him of his mission. Their message, delivered by an eagle, rouses him from his spiritual lethargy and spurs him to defeat the serpent.

I seized the pearl
and turned to carry it to my father.

Those filthy and impure garments
I stripped off, leaving them in the fields,
and went straight on my way
into the light of our homeland in the east.

As in the parable, sin is a distraction and a digression from a path we were set upon in love. But we find that such love itself can be an unexpectedly difficult taskmaster. William Blake wrote that having lived in a heavenly home, we "are put on earth a little space, that we might learn to bear the beams of love." Why should love be something we have to learn to bear? Love can weigh upon us as a burden, like the high expectations of a mentor who knows our potential or the restrictive rules of parents, which are an index of their concern. In these cases, we do indeed need to be schooled in recognizing love for what it is and submit ourselves to its purifying power.

As the crusty Brigham Young put it, "the gospel . . . causes men and women to reveal that which would have slept in their dispositions until they dropped into their graves. The plan by which the Lord leads this people . . . brings out every trait of disposition lurking in their [beings]. . . . Every fault that a person has will be made manifest, that it may be corrected." The crucible by which our spirits grow in stature, and the correction we need along the way, can at times feel insupportable.

A similar paradox is evident in the prophet's admonition, that we "feast upon [Christ's] love; for ye may, *if your minds are firm*, forever." Why should we need firm minds to feast upon love? Like all gifts, love can be hard to receive. As children we welcome presents and affection with the same ready heart and hand, but we tend to lose the knack as we grow older and more self-sufficient. Love may be a heavy burden because of pride; we want to be self-made men and women, paying our own way, and are ashamed of our need. Perhaps we are made to see our own littleness, by the great chasm that opens up between our merit and the gift. Or perhaps we are genuinely ill at ease, as one who knows at what great cost the gift has come.

George Herbert described his discomfort, as only one deeply acquainted with it could.

Love bade me welcome: yet my soul drew back,
Guilty of dust and sin.
But quick-ey'd Love, observing me grow slack
From my first entrance in,
Drew nearer to me, sweetly questioning,
If I lack'd anything.
"A guest," I answer'd, "worthy to be here:"
Love said, "You shall be he."
"I the unkind, ungrateful? Ah my dear,
I cannot look on thee."
Love took my hand, and smiling did reply,
"Who made the eyes but I?"
"Truth Lord, but I have marr'd them: let my shame
Go where it doth deserve."
"And know you not," says Love, "who bore the blame?"
"My dear, then I will serve."
"You must sit down," says Love, "and taste my meat:"
So I did sit, and eat.

The poet learns at last what the Lucifer of Milton's epic poem did not, "that a grateful mind by owing owes not," and that not our righteousness, but His mercy and grace give us a place at the table.

Perhaps, knowing the difficulties in store for those venturing into mortality, we embarked with reservations rather than with the fearless bravado of Robert Frost's heroic legions. Such at least is the version embedded in Jewish legend. According to the Talmud, Gabriel is the angel assigned to bring human souls from the "treasury" where they reside to their point of earthly embarkation. The guide extinguishes the soul's lamp of memory, and when the spirit hesitates (as we all do), Gabriel gives us a flick on the nose. In a gentler version of the tale, the angel places his finger over the spirit's lips as the spirit enters the body, commanding her to forget her premortal past. In both versions, we retain the philtrum, that soft indentation between nose and lips—the mark of the angel. And though the lamp of memory is extinguished, "some weaker rayes" persist to bring us back home, "past the perill of the way."

CHAPTER FOUR

None of Them Is Lost

GOD HAS THE DESIRE AND THE POWER TO UNITE AND EXALT THE ENTIRE HUMAN FAMILY IN A KINGDOM OF HEAVEN, AND EXCEPT FOR THE MOST STUBBORNLY UNWILLING, THAT WILL BE OUR DESTINY.

"This is the father's will . . . that of all which He hath given me I should lose nothing."

God is personally invested in shepherding His children through the process of mortality and beyond; His desires are set upon the whole human family, not upon a select few. He is not predisposed to just the fast learners, the naturally inclined, or the morally gifted. The project of human advancement that God designed offers a hope to the entire human race. It is universal in its appeal and reach alike. This, however, has not been the traditional view.

Some Christians believed hell to be a more populous destination than heaven. The Bible had declared that "the gate is narrow and the road is hard that leads to life, and there are few who find it." Just how few was a matter of recurrent speculation. One popular friar of the early eighteenth century, St. Leonard of Port Maurice, sermonized on "The Little Number of Those Who are Saved," reviewing the opinions of church authorities from St. Augustine and

Thomas Aquinas up to his own day. Most everyone he surveyed agreed that "the greater number of Christian adults are damned." Non-Christians and unbaptized children weren't even possible candidates for salvation. He relates one visionary account that put the proportions at two souls saved and three in purgatory for every thirty-three thousand damned to hell. Another source gave odds of three saved out of sixty thousand.

By mid-eighteenth century, two religious titans of the Anglo-Saxon world, former allies, were publicly debating the question of just how many people were destined for an eternity in hell. In 1738, John Wesley sermonized against the "blasphemy contained in the horrible decree of predestination." His objection was that the doctrine consigned "the greater part of mankind [to] abide in death without any possibility of redemption." Popular preacher George Whitefield published his response in 1740, attacking the idea that "God's grace is free to all." This was tantamount to "propagating the doctrine of universal redemption," he protested, insisting that only a select few were chosen for salvation, while "the rest of mankind . . . will at last suffer that eternal death which is its proper wages."

Whitefield's language raises the question about what kind of thinking underlies our inherited notions about salvation and damnation. We have described our ascent to earth as a costly, sometimes harrowing, education in the school of eternal development. But we know that more than simple error is involved in our mortal experiences. Guilt is a real—and legitimate—human emotion, and it signals that sin is more than an outdated religious concept. With his reference to mankind's "proper wages," Whitefield was alluding to the doctrine of Original Sin, which he accused Wesley of denying. For if we all sinned in Adam, we would all merit damnation in consequence. According to that school of thought, it would be surprising if many were saved and few were damned, not the other way around.

However, if we reject Original Sin and inherited guilt as

unreasonable, then what do we mean by salvation in the first place? Who is in need of rescue, and from what? If life is meant to be educative, and we are learning from our errors, why does the threat of divine retribution loom over our heads? Even if we admit that we are responsible for our own poor choices, why would God punish us for mistakes made along our path to moral growth and betterment?

Job's visitor Elihu asked this same question, trying to fathom the link between Job's behavior and his standing before God. His question still rings loud in our ears: "If you have sinned, what do you accomplish against him? And if your transgressions are multiplied, what do you to him?" Why do our actions, for good or ill, matter to God, in other words, and why would He choose to punish or reward accordingly?

We have already established that God is invested in our lives and happiness, because He chooses to be a Father to us. His concern with human sin is with the pain and suffering it produces. Sympathy and sorrow, not anger and vengeance, are the emotions we must look to in order to plumb the nature of the divine response to sin. In the biblical book of Judges, Israel repeatedly forsakes the worship of Jehovah, and suffers defeat and oppression at their enemies' hands as a result. Eventually, the Israelites repent and cry unto the Lord for mercy. In reply, He reminds them of their recurrent faithlessness.

It is not the injured pride of a tyrant that we see here, but the pain of a suffering parent. "Ye have abandoned me," He responds. Then we read, "and He could no longer bear to see Israel suffer." ("His soul was grieved for the misery of Israel" in the King James Version.) In the language of scripture, this is God's response to human sin, an underlying sorrow, not anger. Sin is pain, and the intensity of His response to sin is commensurate with the intensity of that pain He knows sin will entail, and in which He has already chosen to share. For He is the God who weeps.

Sin itself is a condition we assume when we place ourselves in opposition to those moral laws that undergird the structure of reality. This condition is naturally one of alienation from God, from those we love, and from "the better angels" of our own nature. Sin is not an arbitrary category God imposes. And it is not synonymous with simple error or misjudgment. This is a truth, like others we are examining, that is best revealed in the searchlight of honest introspection. We know the difference between regret and remorse. We regret giving erroneous directions that get the stranger lost. We feel remorse for the slander deliberately spoken. We regret an action that leads to harm. We feel remorse for *choosing* that action to inflict harm. Legitimate guilt, the kind we cannot explain away or therapeutically resolve, involves more than bad judgment or human error. The degree of guilt we experience is proportional to the deliberateness with which we cause hurt. Herein lies the clue to the meaning of sin, and the way beyond it.

The pain associated with sin is the natural consequence of our choices; it is not God's retribution upon the wicked. God grieved over Israel's pain for the same reason Job's friends grieved over his: beloved human beings were suffering, and God's perfect compassion made His participation in their pain inescapable. When Enoch saw God weeping, he learned it was humanity's "misery," the fact of their "suffering," that drew forth heaven's tears. God's mourning for rebellious Israel was for their present misery, not an imagined future hell. The gift and power of agency mean we are free to create the conditions of our own existence—which can be a blessing or a curse.

As an inmate of a concentration camp, Corrie Ten Boom heard a commotion, and saw a short distance away a prison guard mercilessly beating a female prisoner. "What can we do for these people?" Corrie whispered. "Show them that love is greater," Betsie replied. In that moment, Corrie realized her sister's focus was on the prison guard, not the victim she was watching. Betsie saw the world through a different lens. She considered the actions of greatest moral gravity to be the ones we originate, not the ones we suffer.

One of Hollywood's more sublime moments occurs in the classic film, *Lawrence of Arabia*. The British soldier, T. E. Lawrence's only guide across the desert, has been murdered by the Arab Sherif Ali. Ali offers to take the place of the dead Bedouin. Lawrence proudly refuses Ali's offer, insisting he can find his own way with the simple aid of his compass. At this point, an armed Ali snatches his compass, asking, "How if I take it?" Lawrence replies without a pause, "Then you would be a thief."

The unexpected response jolts us because we are not accustomed to consider a death to be less significant than a theft. Unspoken, of course, is Lawrence's real point. Yes, Lawrence would wander helplessly in the desert. He would suffer thirst, fatigue, and exhaustion, followed by a painful, lingering demise. That would be unfortunate, but, as with the prisoner pitied by Corrie ten Boom, his death would be a passing tragedy; by contrast Ali's action, just as the guard's, is a gesture of permanent self-definition. What is always at stake in any decision we make is what that choice turns us into. We may suffer the unfortunate consequences of *other* peoples' choices. People may honor or abuse us, harm or nourish us. But for the most part, it is our *own* choices that shape our identity.

Percy Shelley's mythic hero Prometheus makes the same point in the play *Prometheus Unbound*. Tortured beyond endurance by demonic furies, Prometheus responds to the final vision of pain with which the monsters threaten him, saying, "I weigh not what ye do, but what ye suffer, being evil." This is the tragedy of sin, that we have created for ourselves (as well as for those caught in our path) a condition of pain and suffering. It has not been imposed from without, but is a product of our own choices. The great medieval poet Dante realized this truth hundreds of years ago, when he depicted the most vivid portrait of hell in world literature. No god or demons impel the damned to cross the river Styx to enter into their torments; "they are eager for the river crossing," for their fate is but the natural culmination of their true "desire," expressed through a lifetime of choices.

That is why the characters found in Dante's hell are merely suffering the unfolding, the natural working out, of the decisions freely made in life. Paolo and Francesca, for example, were adulterous lovers. They chose to submit to the winds of passion that incited them to faithlessness; now they are weightless spirits, wafted to and fro eternally by the gusts that blow through hell. As they did not exercise control over their actions on earth, they cannot control the winds that buffet them now. No judge was necessary, and no God decreed their fate. If they are punished, it is a punishment of their own making.

We find this theme repeated throughout the circles of hell. Those who sowed discord and division, find themselves bodily sundered in twain. Despising unity and harmony, they literally inherit the disunity and disharmony upon which they set their hearts. Those who, in the Revelator's words, were neither hot nor cold in life, but pursued a safe, middle path devoid of either good or evil, find themselves eternally in the press of a huge crowd, following a fluttering banner to and fro, never to find a place in hell, and without hope of heaven. Astrologers and false prophets walk eternally with their heads on backwards. Because they chose to look elsewhere than to the real source of truth, so will they forever be barred from approaching whatever truth they now behold. Through examples poignant and playful, Dante drives home the truth that hell is a prison we build for ourselves one brick and one choice at a time.

The experience of sin, then, is not an unalterable state we inhabit; it is a felt disharmony. The unhappiness of sin is nothing more than our spirit rebelling against a condition alien to its true nature. We have fallen out of alignment with ourselves, and with that God whose love we crave and whose nature we share. The separation from God is not a punishment inflicted by God, but the consequence of an existential reality of our own making. We have chosen to exist in a condition "contrary to the nature of God," as an ancient American prophet named Alma explained. We are acting "contrary to the nature of that righteousness" which is the root of God's identity and the source of His perfect joy.

God's supreme happiness is not an arbitrary category of the divine nature; it is inseparable from the perfection of those attributes that He chooses to manifest through His actions—actions that He invites and empowers us to emulate. The alienation in need of repair is not a product of God's arbitrary decree, or His anger or desire to punish. Neither is it purely a matter of human guilt or shame before the Divine Presence. It is a product of a freely chosen sinful condition that is incompatible with God's holiness.

We experience this disharmony as guilt. We can treat guilt as an emotional inconvenience and tolerate or rationalize it until we grow spiritual calluses to deaden the pain. Or, we can treat guilt as a healthy prod to action, as a pain that signifies a deeper injury in need of remedy—an actual injury signifying real spiritual harm. Guilt is what we feel when we have positioned ourselves in opposition to laws and principles that exist eternally and independently of the mind.

Commandments are the expression of those eternal laws that will lead us to a condition of optimal joyfulness. They are the beacon lights of greater realities that define the cosmic streams in which we swim. Operating in harmony with those realities, as a swimmer who works with the current rather than against it, empowers and liberates us to fill the measure of our creation. We may ignore them in the illusion of utter self-sufficiency and independence. But we are then no more than a swimmer thrashing furiously, confident of our powerful strokes, but swept along nevertheless, a captive of the prevailing tides.

In a culture increasingly infatuated with the rhetoric of choice and freedom, we resist the obvious. We find ourselves in a universe pervaded by laws that define the relationship of action and consequence. Some are manmade: speed and you get a ticket; rob and you go to jail; break curfew and you're grounded. Some are physical: let go of a rock and it drops; expose potassium to air and it forms hydrogen gas; mix baking soda and vinegar and you get a frothing pot worthy of the witch's concoction in Shakespeare's *Macbeth*. And some laws are moral: nurturing hatred cankers the soul; practicing kindness and forbearance develops serenity.

Parents and police officers alert us to the first category. Physicists and chemists may give us fluency in the second. But nothing short of trial and error will convert us to the unyielding strictures of the third. To be adept at the first entails outward behavior. Mastering the second challenges our mind. But to live in harmony with the moral law of the universe requires body and soul, heart and mind, the will and the affections of the undivided self. This is the meaning of Jesus' words that living the highest and holiest law, loving God, requires "all your heart, and . . . all your soul, and . . . all your mind."

For this kind of education, nothing short of total immersion in a world of choice and consequence will suffice, and sin is one of those consequences. No other path to perfection is possible, as Julian of Norwich learned. "I thought, if sin had not been, we should all be clean and like our Lord, as He made us. And thus in my folly, . . . often I wondered why, by God's wisdom and foresight, He did not prevent sin." And then the answer came to her, that "sin is behovely" [necessary and beneficial], but "all shall be well, and all shall be well, and all manner of things shall be well."

Only by choosing the good and experiencing its fruit do we learn to savor and embrace the good. Similarly, only by choosing the evil and living through its consequences do we learn what evil is and why it deserves to be rejected. Or as Julian saw, "So pain endures for a time. Its role is to purge us, make us know ourselves, and it drives us to the Lord." Therein lies the "needfulness" of sin, the part it has to play.

The first woman philosopher in England, Anne Conway, reasoned the same way. "Every sin will have its own punishment and every creature will feel pain and chastisement, which will return that creature to the pristine state of goodness in which it was created and from which it can never fall again because, through its punishment, it has acquired a greater perfection and strength. . . . Hence, one can infer that all God's creatures . . . must be changed and restored after a certain time to a condition which is not simply as good as that in which they were created, but better."

The question is, having established that we are the products of our own choices, and that they are etched into our very identity and determine our destiny, how do we step off the train, to attain that "better condition"? How do we create a new self, a new trajectory, and a new future? The simple truth is that we are imperfect beings, possessed of imperfectly developed wills, confronting a world constructed as an arena of challenge, opposition, and temptation.

The very real detritus of lives tainted by selfishness, ambition, and pride constitute the prison of sin in which we entomb ourselves. The burden of sin that has become habit, the self-perpetuating spiral of choices that further compromise our will and weaken our resolve, a character impaired by the accumulation of soul-damaging decisions, all conspire to make our predicament seem hopeless. In protesting his mother's evil actions, Hamlet begs her to change her course, telling her the freedom to change still operates where habit is not yet set in stone. "Let me wring your heart," he pleads, "for I shall, if it be made of penetrable stuff; if damned custom have not brazed it so, that it be proof and bulwark against sense."

Most human hearts, we find, are made of penetrable stuff. Several catalysts to change open to our possible futures. We may find we are simply fatigued with the world, discovering its satisfactions so far beneath our expectations. "As long as I can conceive something better than myself I cannot be easy unless I am striving to bring it into existence," says one of George Bernard Shaw's characters. It may be simple love of others that motivates us to live kinder, gentler lives. Or it may be, as Clement of Alexandria believed, the *memory* of a more joy-filled way, "the recollection of what is better," that leads us to repent "for what is worse," retrace our steps, and "speed back to the eternal light, children to the Father."

Such intimations may be the impetus we need to examine our behavior and its consequences, in order to change, to align ourselves with principles of happiness, "the object and design" of our existence. We cannot ourselves transcend the consequences of our own past choices, or suddenly acquire a new human nature unshaped by our own history. The inevitability of sin means the inevitability of sinful habits and consequent alienation from God and His heaven. In His infinite love and compassion, however, God wills the reintegration of *every* individual into the Heavenly Family. The human freedom to sin thus collides with God's desire to exalt and bless. The problem of how to reconcile this tragic collision is the problem of atonement, by which we mean, full and harmonious reconciliation. Any solution, any version of at-one-ment or reconciliation to God, must bring all who sojourn on earth back to God's presence, but must do so without violating human agency.

Genuine moral agency entails necessary consequences. Choice is always choice of something. In John Stuart Mill's classic treatment of the subject, human liberty requires the freedom "of doing as we like, *subject to such consequences as may follow.*" Those consequences may look like punishment or reward from our perspective, but they were *chosen*. That is how freedom operates, ideally at least. Consequences are chosen at the time actions are freely committed. To choose to indulge a desire is to choose its fruit—bitter or sweet—assuming, and this is a crucial caveat—that "men are instructed sufficiently" to understand what they are choosing.

Clearly, instruction is never perfect, the playing field is never entirely even, and a host of mitigating circumstances complicate and constrain the agency that humans exercise. We never operate on the basis of perfect understanding; we are never entirely free of social, cultural, and biological influences. Secondhand smoke of a thousand types complicates and compromises the degree of freedom and accountability behind human choice.

The underlying principle, however, does not vary: we are becoming what we love and desire. Ralph Waldo Emerson wrote, "We may think our tribute is paid in secret in the dark recesses of our hearts, but it will out. That which dominates our imaginations and our thoughts will determine our lives, and our character. . . . What we are worshipping we are becoming." Every moment of every day our choices enact our loves, our desires, and our aspirations. And we are molding ourselves into the God or gods we thereby worship.

That is why all talk about punishment and rewards, about justice and merit and deserts, can be wrongheaded and misleading. We are not in some contest to rack up points. We will not someday wait with bated breath to see what prize or pain is meted out by a great dispenser of trophies. We cannot so trivialize life that we make of it a coliseum where we wage moral combat like spiritual gladiators, for a presiding Authority on high to save or damn according to our performance. Where would be the purpose in all that? He might take the measure of our souls at any moment and deal with us accordingly, saving Himself, not to mention us, a great deal of trouble.

How much more meaningful is a life designed for spiritual formation, rather than spiritual evaluation. All tests evaluate, and life is no exception. But the most meaningful and productive tests are those that assess with an eye to improvement, that measure in order to remedy, and that improve and prepare us for the next stage in an upward process of advancement. For these reasons, all talk of heaven that operates in terms of earning rather than becoming is misguided. Such ideas misconstrue the nature of God, His grace, and the salvation He offers.

The English minister William Law found himself "incapable of thinking otherwise of God than as the one . . . who can will nothing else to all eternity, but to communicate good, and blessing, and happiness, and perfection to every life, according to its capacity to receive it. Had I a hundred lives, I could with more ease part with them all by suffering a hundred deaths than give up this lovely idea of God."

Law correctly apprehended the nature of the weeping God of Enoch, and with these words he has revealed the key to the whole question of a restrictive heaven. Why, in other words, can a merciful God not simply open the gates to all and sundry? Humans can remit a penalty out of compassion or mercy—even when wrong is not acknowledged and forgiveness not asked; why cannot God do the same? Because only a simpleminded conception of heaven, as an exclusive celestial club with literal gates and wary porters, admits of such a question.

Heaven is not a club we enter. Heaven is a state we attain, in accordance with our "capacity to receive" a blessed and sanctified nature. A nineteenth-century scripture dictated by Joseph Smith echoed Law's point in similar language. Describing the disposition of people after death, the visionary account reveals that some spirits "shall return again to their own place, to enjoy that which they are *willing to receive*, because they were not willing to enjoy that which they might have received." In other words, we acquire Heaven in accordance with a growing capacity to receive it.

What we conclude at this point is this: God cannot arbitrarily dispense a blanket "salvation" on the human race for two reasons. First, because heaven depends on our attaining a particular mode of being, a character and mind and will that are the product of lifelong choosing. Conforming to celestial laws, we become celestial persons. "That which is governed by law is also preserved by law and perfected and sanctified by the same," in the language of scripture. Salvation, in this light, is the imitation of Christ—or, to make the concept clearer, the *imitating* of Christ. One is only merciful to the extent one *extends* mercy. One is only honest to the extent one *practices* honesty. One is only truthful to the extent one *speaks* truthfully, and so on. That is why, all good intentions and Christ's grace notwithstanding, whosoever chooses "to abide in sin, . . . *cannot* be sanctified by law, neither by mercy." Heaven is a *condition* and a sanctified *nature* toward which all godly striving tends; it is not a place to be found by walking through the right door with a heavenly hall pass.

There is a second reason our salvation cannot be simply awarded by divine decree. Even if it were possible, imposing a heavenly reward on those who do not choose heaven would be just that: an imposition on the "unwilling" and an abrogation of the moral agency on which all human life and earthly existence is predicated. It is because of the sanctity of choice that "we have no claim . . . in relation to Eternal things unless our actions & contracts & all things tend to this end." We cannot expect heaven if we do not *choose* heaven, in simplest terms. This view of salvation does not preempt Christ's grace. The opportunity to follow in Christ's mold is utterly predicated upon a grace of which Christ's death on the cross is the most supernal, but neither the first nor the final, instance. All of which takes us back to our earlier question: how can God rescue us from the prison of our own damaged will, and help us transcend the condition our poor choices—and out and out sins—have brought us to, without abrogating our agency?

We never feel the full brunt of our own choices, and we are never left to bear the full consequences of our own sinful behavior. What would normally be a self-perpetuating process leading from self-concern to self-absorption to self-obsession is interrupted, by a call to nobler things. A tenuous connection to the divine persists, a reaching after, tender mercies that call us back from the precipice, and beckon us to change course. One finds, wrote the psychologist William James, "that the tenderer parts of [our] personal life" connect us to a source of infinite tenderness "which is operative in the world outside" ourselves; a source that we "can keep in working touch with, and in a fashion get on board of . . . when all [our] lower being has gone to pieces in the wreck."

These intimations of grace, these hints of a doom deflected, bear record of consequences that someone else has borne, pains another has suffered, where we ought to have. The atonement of Jesus Christ, His agony in Gethsemane and His death on the cross, is the only action by which the wounds of sin and hurt that rend the world can be repaired. The words of Isaiah describe the "suffering servant's" mission: "to bind up the brokenhearted, to proclaim liberty to the captives, and the opening of the prison to them that are bound; . . . to comfort all that mourn; to appoint unto them that mourn in Zion, to give unto them beauty for ashes, the oil of joy for mourning, the garment of praise for the spirit of heaviness."

This great healing of the universe is centered on the breach in our relationship with our God. That relationship is the most important one in which we participate. In some measure this is because it is the foundation of all human relationships of which we are a part, and which are impaired and crippled by sin. The majesty and mystery of Christ's sacrifice have the palpable impact of eternal consequence, though we have only glimmers of understanding. There is a logic to the power of the Atonement, if no certainty as to its workings.

What we do know is that on a hillside outside Jerusalem's city wall, two millennia ago, the man known to history as Jesus of Nazareth, and adored by His followers as the Son of God, submitted to be executed by a protracted, agonizing death on a cross. "I lay down my life for the sheep," He said. "And I, when I am lifted up from the earth, will draw *all* people to myself." His death was a willing sacrifice that secured immortality for man. When He rose from the dead on Easter morning He was the first fruits of a universal resurrection He only could usher in. Endless life is no boon by itself, however. God's purpose is to give us not mere existence in the eternities, but "an abundant life," a life fully like His own. His design is not to extend our life indefinitely, but to enhance it permanently. That is why atonement involves much more than Christ's death on a cross.

Jesus told His disciples that His blood was specifically "poured out for many for the forgiveness of sins." In the moments before His physical torments commenced on Calvary, the evangelist describes the incomprehensible anguish of soul that Christ suffered. As He collapsed under the compounded weight of human sin and sorrow, "an angel from heaven appeared to him and gave him strength. In his anguish he prayed more earnestly, and his sweat became like great drops of blood falling down on the ground." The garden was aptly named; Gethsemane means place of the olive press, where "Ev'n God himself [was] pressed for my sake."

What can it mean, that Christ's blood was spilt for our sins, that "by his bruises we are healed"? Perhaps His perfect love means His identification with human suffering is so complete, that in one fell vision He comprehended the depth and range and terror of all our individual pain. Perhaps it is the almost irresistible power of His superabundant love manifest in His choice to suffer what He suffered, that transforms the sinner's heart.

In some way He deflected the consequences of our own sinful choices, absorbing them Himself, willingly suffering the alienation even from His Father that His fearful words on the cross signified. Thereby He upholds and affirms human agency, by ensuring consequences follow choice—and we witness how terrible they can be, without ourselves experiencing their full onslaught. Somehow He "suffered these things for all, that they might not suffer if they would repent." In some manner and by some mechanism that the scriptures decline to explicate, Christ suffered for, on behalf of, on account of, and in the stead of, us. The question, however, remains: on what basis can the consequences of our choices be deferred or abated?

The law of moral agency, of choice and consequence, does not require that we entirely bear the burden of our own choices made in this life because those choices are always made under circumstances that are less than perfect. Our accountability is thus always partial, incomplete. Into that gap between choice and accountability, the Lord steps. Christ's atonement provides a way to break the cycle of sin, and begin a new life-course (in ways large or small) with a newly forged disposition. Growing in the hard-won knowledge of good and evil, we are better able to choose in the greater light of a fuller understanding, or with a more unencumbered will.

The Greek term, *metanoia*, means a change or reversal of mind, purpose, or disposition. Repentance, in other words, means to re-decide, to choose afresh. But the mercy thus freely offered through Christ's atonement, His gesture of supernal grace, cannot extend to the point of choosing on behalf of individuals. Repentance is therefore an ongoing process by which we repudiate unrighteous choices, acknowledging Christ's role in suffering the consequences of those sins on our behalf, and choosing afresh in accordance with purified desire. And so we go on choosing, again and again. The process continues—perhaps aeons into the future—until in perfect harmony with the laws that underlie the nature of happiness (and thus the nature of God), we have reached a sanctified condition that permits a perfect at-one-ment with God. God's desire to save is reconciled with the sanctity of human choice. Love and agency, justice and mercy, meet.

At least, that is the hope Christ's atonement holds out for us. How many, in actual fact, will be partakers of the feast to which they are invited? Was Wesley or Whitefield right about the proportion of the blessed and the damned? The answer hinges on what we consider to be the time frame, and the circumstances, under which repentance and moral growth can occur. Exactly who, in other words, is eligible for heaven?

One reason for the horrifying statistics cited by the eighteenth-century friar was the understanding, commonplace from the Middle

Ages forward, that two enormous classes of humanity were outside the saving grace of Christ: unbaptized infants, and non-Christians. For many centuries, Christian theologians defended the inscrutable justice of God and cared little for making His harsher decrees palatable to humans. But condemning biblical figures from Adam to Abraham, who happened to be born before the era of Christian hope, seemed patently wrong even to the most stalwart defenders of orthodoxy, so exceptions were made for them. Museums are full of paintings by the masters, depicting Christ leading a line of bearded patriarchs out through the underworld's gates, in what theologians called "the harrowing of hell."

Whitefield correctly saw that compromise could not be reached on this point without a radical reformulation of foundational precepts—such as Original Sin. Meanwhile, Wesley agonized over "How uncomfortable a thought is this, that thousands and millions of men, without any preceding offence or fault of theirs were unchangeably doomed to everlasting burnings!" He and others considered that unbaptized children could not be guilty before they had attained moral awareness—but what about the legions of those who had never heard of Christ or His gospel in the first place?

Most Christians have gradually come to agree that little children are not guilty of Adam's sin—or their own sins until they are old enough to be morally responsible. In 2007, the Catholic Church claimed "serious theological and liturgical grounds for hope that unbaptized infants who die will be saved." But that leaves two problems unaddressed. First, to exempt children from sin is not the same thing as to accord them an opportunity to grow and progress, to acquire the understanding, embrace those principles, and practice the virtue, that constitute true goodness and happiness. Godliness, sanctification, the imitation of Christ, all presuppose more than the absence of sin; perfection itself, as its Middle English roots remind us, means "completeness," not just freedom from blemish. How does mere absolution from an Adamic inheritance itself integrate an individual into a process of profound transformation and progress?

This takes us back to our earlier point about how limiting, confining, and ultimately unhelpful is a model that sees damnation as our default condition, and simple rescue as the solution. Rescuing children from a condition they didn't deserve and never really inherited in the first place doesn't reveal a great deal about the meaning of their eternal nature, their brief lives, or their future possibilities.

Second, if it is not fair to consign children to hell because of their incapacity to either embrace or reject Christ and His teachings, neither does it make any moral sense to believe those never exposed to Christ and His teachings, or to any moral framework at all, would be consigned to hell—or lack the opportunity to grow toward heaven. Surely an infant is the most deserving object of our compassion, and therefore of God's compassion. If any justice reigns on high, it seems, unbaptized infants would not be punished for dying before having the opportunity to accept Christ and His gospel.

The larger problem, however, is that vastly more people have lived, and will always live, outside the orbit of Christianity, never hearing a sermon, seeing a missionary, or reading a Bible, than have died in infancy. The multitudes that covered the earth before Christianity made its appearance, all the inhabitants of nations past, present, and future where Christianity is virtually unknown, the countless children reared in secular homes—the numbers of these uncatechized throngs dwarf the number of children who have died unbaptized. The largest portion of humanity would still fall outside the gospel's reach.

And, as with the children, the problem facing the non-Christian runs deeper than anything a simple blanket amnesty can resolve. The question isn't whether they can be excused or forgiven, in light of their ignorance. The point is not that all humans are condemned unless they find a compelling excuse. The issue, rather, is that all come to earth in order to participate in an educative and transformative process. If the whole mission of Christ and His atonement is to enable change, to render repentance and personal transformation possible, to empower and sanctify, then what are we to say about the billions who have lived in obliviousness to such power and grace? The question is not how can they be rescued from damnation, but how can they be elevated or ennobled, given their inability to participate in all that His grace makes possible?

We must recognize at this juncture that only two options were ever really on the table. The first is that Christ and His gospel do uniquely empower us on our path to perfection and immortality; Christ really does embody the solution to the twin barriers to human progression: sin and death. The second possibility is that Christ and His sacrifice are not really the unique means of furthering God's plans for humankind. If the latter is the case, then the entire Christian enterprise is well intentioned but not of vital importance. Valuable perhaps across a spectrum of societal and personal functions—from famine relief to community building to moral improvement and psychological consolation—but ultimately, when all is said and done and the earth has come and gone, inessential and incapable of fulfilling its own promises.

If, on the other hand, the first is the case, then the enormous efforts legions of missionaries and evangelizers have expended through the centuries to execute the "Great Commission," to preach the gospel to all nations, tongues, kindreds, and peoples makes sense. In fact, no enterprise could be a more worthwhile undertaking. But these efforts are obviously woefully inadequate to the task of redeeming the whole of humankind. Christians are supposed to believe that Christ and His gospel are essential to mankind's eternal growth and happiness, but admit at the outset that the overwhelming majority of the human family will be forever handicapped by the accidents of history, cut off from eternal happiness because of when and where they were born?

Offering the hope of an amnesty for infants while ignoring the rest of humanity represents a rather limited defense of God's mysterious justice. It also suggests that His plan was not very effective to begin with, limited as it was to such a relatively small pool of humanity. God seems scarcely deserving of His title if this is the case. Such a God would be severely lacking in either the desire to promote a universal happiness, or the capacity to do so.

So we have a dilemma. Granting opportunity only to those who accept Christ in the flesh seems patently unfair and inefficient. Giving amnesty to all the rest of humankind makes of Christ's life and sacrifice a magnificent gesture but a superfluous or redundant one. A reasonable conception of God and His plan for us demands a third possibility.

In the early Christian centuries, Origen had taught that God would somehow find a way to redeem all of His children from the effects of sin. He never worked out the details of how that would come about, and his belief in "universal salvation" was soon declared a heresy. For centuries heaven seemed sealed shut against all save the elect, or the fortunate few believers. By the eighteenth century, the same impulse that increasingly resisted a decree of universal damnation, was in some quarters returning to Origen's vision of a universal redemption.

Some Christians organized themselves around just such a belief. "God, whose nature is Love, . . . will finally restore the whole family of mankind to holiness and happiness," proclaimed one group in 1790. He would never have created the human race, argued the influential Charles Chauncy, "unless He intended to make them finally happy." His infinite wisdom, patience, and compassion would succeed, eventually, in persuading even the most recalcitrant to accept His mercy.

This generous vision still left unaddressed the question of how the multitudes that died outside the Christian pale—or before baptism—would be fitted for eternal life. The general solution clearly had to extend into the life to come beyond the veil of death. "'Tis true," Chauncy conceded, God "will not, in this state, prevail upon all willingly to bow down before Him as their Lord. . . . May He not, . . . use means with sinners in the next state, in order to make them good subjects in the moral kingdom of God?"

Charles Beecher thought such a third way was the only reasonable alternative to mass damnation on the one hand, and a superfluous atonement on the other. A more comprehensive program than the one executed by missionaries among the living must be envisioned. In 1863, he was convicted of heresy for such a belief. The ecclesiastical court ruled that Beecher "weakens and undermines the doctrine of future punishment by teaching that the offers of salvation are made to men *after* death."

Beecher's position is the only reasonable one. If hearing and believing the message of Christ is essential to all mankind's eternal happiness, then that opportunity must be available beyond the confines of mortal life. Why not, asked missionary Parley Pratt, insisting the dead "not only live, move, and think but might hear the gospel. . . . We reason from what we know." In the "spirit world societies are made up of all kinds." Many presumably "have lived in part of the spirit world . . . where the key has not yet been turned nor the gospel preached." If this is true, then the fact would explain Peter's claim that "the gospel was preached also to them that are dead, that they might be judged according to men in the flesh, but live according to God in the spirit."

Peter's cryptic allusion represents the Christian Bible's single most stupendous moment of liberality and generosity. The eighteenth-century revolt against organized religion was in large measure a protest against the narrowness of its vision. As the philosopher and author Gotthold Lessing phrased it, "accidental truths of history can never become the proof of necessary truths of reason." What he meant was, God could not hide the Savior's advent in a Bethlehem stable, and require all humans across time and cultures to recognize its universal import. Paul's words suggest an original conception of a ministry that would extend not just across borders, but across death itself.

The belief that the work of ministry includes the departed, animates the Latter-day Saint practice of tracing the roots of their families into ages past and performing gospel ordinances on their behalf. "The work of love in remembering one who is dead is a work of the utmost unselfish love," wrote the Danish philosopher Søren Kierkegaard. "If one wants to make sure that love is completely unselfish, he eliminates every possibility of repayment. But precisely this is eliminated in the relationship to one who is dead. If love nevertheless remains, it is in truth unselfish."

Referring to the performance of sacraments on behalf of the deceased, Krister Stendahl expressed "holy envy" for a practice so conspicuously rooted in love for one's ancestors. We see in this undertaking, with its hints of ancient origins (1 Cor. 15:29), acts of devotion performed across a veil of silence, a reaching after our dead in the hope of uniting them to us.

If we are serious about our prospects of life beyond the grave, then we should not shy away from making a considered effort to understand what kinds of continuity with this life make sense. If God's dominion does not end with our death, why should the progress of the human soul? The particular potency of the challenges we face—our bodily weakness, the instincts and passions that consume us, the press of evil all around us—make a life of virtuous aspiration very like a race through quicksand. However, it is just these conditions of mortality, like the world of Darwin's honeybee, that are especially conducive to growth and progress.

Life may well give us, in a concentrated dose, the soul-stretching most necessary to our long-range spiritual development. That would explain the urgency for acting in the here and now to pursue the path of virtue. For those with the understanding and capacity, procrastinating repentance does not just prolong our pain and forestall our happiness; it may greatly prolong and complicate the process when repentance does begin. But even for those who live and die in obliviousness to God's eternal purposes, death does not freeze the soul in time.

In God's universe nothing is stationary. For the last two centuries, we have known that the stars and planets are not arrayed in a perfect celestial order, a once and forever system of static harmony. When William Herschel plied his magnificent telescopes in the late 1700s, he observed a universe in process of continual disruption, upheaval, and transformation on a colossal scale. As suns died and faded away in one quadrant of the galaxy, whole star systems sprang into being in another. If God takes as much care with the destinies of human souls as with the planets they inhabit, surely they too gain in splendor and glory through the cycles of eternity.

What challenges and conditions may come when we have passed into that undiscovered country, death, we cannot know. What we do know is that Jesus spoke in simple, hopeful terms about the people for whom He died. "This is the father's will . . . that of all which He hath given me I should lose nothing, but raise it up again at the last day." Surely, the work of redeeming and exalting that He began before the earth was formed will continue after it passes away.

In the language of conventional Christianity, will all be saved? Put another way, will anyone be eternally consigned to hell? If our intended destiny is to become like our Father in Heaven, "joint-heirs with Christ," then anything short of that eventuality is damnation. As cycles of poor choices may tend ever downward in mortality, so may they hereafter. For redemption to be permanently beyond reach, however, one would have to *choose* to put oneself beyond reach.

Hell, in the sense of permanent alienation from God, a stunting of one's infinite potential, must exist as an option if freedom is to exist. That anyone would choose such a fate is hard to imagine, and yet some of us choose our own private hells often enough in the here and now. The difference is that at present we see "through a glass darkly."

Our decisions are often made in weakness, or with deficient will or understanding. We live on an uneven playing field, where to greater or lesser degree the weakness of the flesh, of intellect, or of judgment intrudes. Poor instruction, crushing environment, chemical imbalances, deafening white noise, all cloud and impair our judgment.

Hardly ever, then, is a choice made with perfect, uncompromised freedom of the will. That, we saw, is why repentance is possible in the first place. We repent when upon reflection, with a stronger will, clearer insight, or deeper desire, we wish to choose differently. To be outside the reach of forgiveness and change, one would have to choose evil, to reject the love of a vulnerable God and His suffering son, in the most absolute and perfect light of understanding, with no impediments to the exercise of full freedom. It is not that repentance would not be allowable in such circumstances; repentance would simply not be conceivable. No new factor, no new understanding, no suddenly healed mind or soul, could abruptly appear to provide a basis for reconsideration or regret.

For us lesser mortals, who never attain such lofty heights of intellect and will, repentance and change continue as long as our striving does. God would not have commanded us to forgive each other seventy times seven, if He were not prepared to extend to us the same mathematical generosity. He seems determined to demonstrate that when we make regrettable choices we are not really choosing what the "better angels of our nature" want to choose. Come, try again, He seems to be saying, like a patient tutor who knows his student's mind is too frozen with fear to add the sums correctly.

Why else would the Lord's strategies be so rife with interventions and second chances? Samuel was called three times in the night, before he recognized his Lord. It took a bright light and a voice from heaven to capture Saul's attention. Who knows how many other potential disciples will find their road to Damascus only on the other side of life's veil? Why should God not there as well as here persist in His efforts to gather His children, as a hen its chicks? Why not believe that "His hand is stretched out still?" If we fall short of salvation, it will be because our cumulative choices, our freely made decision to reject His rescue, have put us beyond His reach, not because His patience has expired.

The idea is certainly a generous one, and it seems suited to the weeping God of Enoch, the God who has set His heart upon us. If some inconceivable few will persist in rejecting the course of eternal progress, they are "the only ones" who will be damned, taught Joseph Smith. "All the rest" of us will be rescued from the hell of our private torments and subsequent alienation from God. "All except" the intractable will be saved, for God will force no man to heaven.

The book of Malachi ends with a cryptic prophecy of Elijah's return to the earth, when He will "turn the hearts of parents to their children and the hearts of children to their parents, so that [the Lord] will not come and strike the land with a curse." Jewish tradition, full of anticipation and yearning, weaves this interpretation: At the coming of the great judgment day, "the children . . . who had to die in infancy will be found among the just, while their fathers will be ranged on the other side. The babes will implore their fathers to come to them, but God will not permit it. Then Elijah will go to the little ones, and teach them how to plead in behalf of their fathers. They will stand before God and say, 'Is not the measure of good, the mercy of God, larger than the measure of chastisements? . . . [May they] be permitted to join us in Paradise?' God will give assent to their pleadings, and Elijah will have fulfilled the word of the prophet Malachi; He will have brought back the fathers to the children."

The beauty of this story is in its intimation that any conception of heaven worth pursuing is inseparable from reconciliation—not just to God, but also to our loved ones, those of our household and those of generations past. One might even read this prophecy, as indeed we do, as suggesting that the living may co-participate in the ongoing work of human redemption. We do not just share good tidings with the living. We can seek out our ancestors in a gesture of remembrance and respect, pray for their welfare, perform on their behalf those sacred ordinances that signify their participation in the family of Christ.

If Christ truly preached to the spirits who had in former days upon the earth been disobedient, then it makes sense to assume that the great work of ministry continues there. We find it reasonable to believe, along with Paul, that "neither death, nor life, nor angels, nor rulers, nor things present, nor things to come, nor powers, nor heights, nor depth, nor anything else in all creation, will be able to separate us from the love of God." One is reminded here of the poet's plea that "God, lover of souls," will "complete thy creature dear O where it fails, / Being mighty . . . , being a father and fond."

As a mighty God, He has the capacity to save us all. As a fond father, He has the desire to do so. That is why, as Smith taught, "God hath made a provision that every spirit can be ferretted out in that world" that has not deliberately and definitively chosen to resist a grace that is stronger than the cords of death.

CHAPTER FIVE

Participants in the Divine Nature

Heaven will consist of those relationships that matter most to us now.

"That you may become participants in the divine nature."

The quest for heaven has always been fraught with danger and ambiguity. The exhilarating recognition that humans may have a kinship with the gods occurs in the oldest religious texts known. The unsettling fear that such dreams of divinity are dangerous occurs with similar frequency. Icarus flew too close to the sun, and plunged to his death. Lucifer said he would "raise [his] throne above the stars of God," and lost his high rank and place alike. The people of Babel aspired to "build a tower with its top in the heavens," and were scattered and linguistically confounded in consequence. Making "a name for ourselves," has always held irresistible appeal.

Typical of the hedge against such pretensions, we find a writer such as Kierkegaard, who affirms as a foundational tenet in Western religious thought the "infinite qualitative difference" between God and man, a distinction of unimaginable and unbridgeable distance.

Another religious scholar held that "the deepest and most fundamental element in all . . . religious devotion" is the feeling that what we worship "lies altogether outside what can be thought, and is, alike in form, quality, and essence, the utterly and 'wholly other.'"

Augustine even repented of his "incredible folly in which I asserted that I was by nature what [God is]." Ambiguity sneaks into the picture when we remember that the same Bible that calls God "the most high," "the Almighty," whose works are wondrous and whose knowledge is perfect, also says we are made in His image and likeness. The God of Genesis who created the heavens and earth, also placed in Eden a tree that offered a way "to become as" He is. The same Christ whom God "highly exalted," exhorted His disciples to follow Him, and to be perfect, as His Father is. To the Ephesians, the New Testament writer summarized simply: "Be imitators of God." John could only marvel at the promise and the mystery: "Beloved, we are God's children now; what we will be has not yet been revealed. What we do know is this: when He is revealed, we will be like Him."

Plato, the father of Western philosophy, believed our paramount moral duty was "becoming like god so far as is possible" and was certain that to do so was to honor, not to blaspheme against, the Divine. Genuine love always desires the highest good for the objects of its affection. We think his words on this subject are among the most inspired ever spoken in the ancient world, even if they originated in a culture far removed from the traditions of Judeo-Christianity. "He who framed this whole universe . . . was good, and one who is good can never become jealous of anything. And so, being free of jealousy, he wanted everything to become as much like himself as was possible."

Plato anticipated, if he did not know, the God described by Paul, who taught that as children of God the Father, we are poised to one day become joint heirs with God the Son. Joseph Addison wrote, "It must be a project pleasing to God Himself, to see His creation for ever beautifying in His eyes, and drawing nearer to him, by greater degrees of resemblance." As long as it is God's nature and character we are striving to emulate, and not His power and glory, we are on safe ground. As the apostle Peter recognized, the "precious and very great promises" given to us are that we "may become participants of the divine nature."

What is this nature many of us seek to emulate? What do we mean by this imitation of Christ? As we saw in Enoch's encounter with God, the principal attribute of the Divine is love—costly love. Witnessing God's weeping over His children is only half the journey Enoch makes. What transpires next to the prophet may be the only—it is surely the most vivid—example given in scripture of what the actual process of acquiring the divine nature requires. It is certainly a lesson far more sobering than exhilarating, a greater call to meekness than grandiosity of spirit.

As Enoch plumbs the mystery of the weeping God, he learns just what it means to be like Him. Seeking insight and understanding into eternal things, Enoch is raised to a perspective from which he sees the world through God's eyes. The experience is more shattering than reassuring: "And it came to pass that the Lord spake unto Enoch, and told Enoch all the doings of the children of men; wherefore Enoch *knew*, and looked upon their wickedness, and their misery, and wept and stretched forth his arms, and his heart swelled wide as eternity; and his bowels yearned; and all eternity shook."

Taught of highest things by the weeping God, Enoch becomes the weeping prophet. His experience of the love that is indiscriminate in its reach and vulnerable in its consequences takes him to the heart of the divine nature. This is the mystery of godliness that Enoch does not just see, but now lives for himself.

Enoch's encounter with God, his vicarious experience of infinite love, serves as a template for the path to heaven he—and all of us—hope to follow. That this path has as its end a communal heaven, and not a solitary salvation, is clear by the vision's end.

In the midst of Enoch's pain, God commands him to "Lift up your heart, and be glad; and look." Only then does he see "the day of the coming of the Son of Man." Recognizing in Christ's advent the great work of healing and redemption, "his soul rejoiced."

At the last day, the ultimate consolation, and the shape of heaven, are revealed. God's righteousness will "sweep the earth as with a flood, to gather out" those who will have Him to be their God. Then, the Lord says to Enoch, "thou and all thy city [shall] meet them there, and we will receive them into our bosom, and they shall see us; and we will fall upon their necks, and they shall fall upon our necks, and we will kiss each other; And there shall be mine abode, and it shall be Zion."

The beauty and power of this image is in its concreteness. God and His people, the living and the departed, heaven and earth, embrace. The immense distance between the spiritual and the mundane collapses, and we find holiness in the ordinary. Luke's tale of the prodigal son turns out to be not symbolic foreshadowing, but literal foretaste, of a greater reunion. As the evangelist told the story, when the son "was yet a great way off, his father saw him, and had compassion, and ran, and fell on his neck, and kissed him."

In Enoch's vision, heaven shocks by its familiarity. God, it would appear, is first and foremost a relational Being, and the heaven toward which we aspire consists of loving relationships that are eternal. God's title as Father is universally acknowledged throughout the Judeo-Christian traditions, but how that title is understood varies widely. We find an understanding that moves in the direction of a literal, familial relationship is more reasonable than one that emphasizes the metaphorical or figurative. Given the eternal nature of the soul, our prior existence in a "first estate" in God's presence, the "qualitative distance" separating man from God may be great, but it is not infinite.

The common view today is that the traditional family is an earthly institution that evolved largely in response to sociocultural or economic forces and motives. It is true that family composition and roles have changed over time. But given our relationship with God that preceded the Creation, the family may be said to have origins just as old. In this sense, one may say "the earthly is the image of the heavenly." In other words, "that which is earthly conform[s] to that which is heavenly," or "that which is temporal [is] in the likeness of that which is spiritual," not just the other way around.

When God created man and woman, He brought them together. That a man should cling to his wife and she to him, on the way to becoming "one flesh," was a pattern and order He established while they were still in paradise. It was not a compensating comfort for their passage through a fallen world, but a sacramental union established in paradise, and anticipating no end. Marriage is a heavenly order, modeled on a divine template—a relationship that may be sealed on earth, in order to be "bound in heaven." "Divine families encircled by his fire and light are the very essence of life and eternal life; without them this earth—indeed this cosmos—will have missed the measure of its creation."

A heavenly society ranges far beyond the domestic. In Christ's great intercessory prayer, offered in the privacy and intimacy of the last supper, rather than the public arena of the Sermon on the Mount, Christ asked God to bless His disciples with a friendship, a love and unity, that paralleled His own relationship to His Father. "The glory that you have given me I have given them," he prayed, "*so that they may be one, as we are one*." No mystical blurring of persons or unity of substance was intended here, but the perfect harmony of heart and mind. The same unity that, tellingly, He referred to elsewhere. "And the Lord called his people Zion, because they were of one heart, and one mind." That is the great mystery, that is really no mystery.

What God envisions for us, what His Son prayed most earnestly for toward the end of His life, was for us to achieve the harmony He shares with His Father. In essence, we are invited to participate in the heavenly family of God Himself. Not through metaphorical melding, but through the studied, arduous practice of a holy life that prepares us to love as He does. Pratt wrote that "our natural affections . . . are the very main-springs of life and happiness—they are the cement of all virtuous and heavenly society. . . . From this union of affection, spring all the other relationships, social joys and affections, diffused through every branch of human existence. Man was designed for a social being."

A child we knew wanted an ant farm. Year after year, he asked for—and received—an ant farm. Left to his own devices, he would happily hasten outside, collect cupfuls of black ants (red ones were too fierce), and carefully place them in their plastic city. And then he would sit back and watch them—over the next few days—wander aimlessly, dwindle, and die. He was never one to read directions, and his dad was not one to supervise childish projects. Only years later did he realize he needed to order a queen ant, so they could all function as a community.

Ants, like bees and termites, are social. They cannot survive individually. The philosopher Aristotle famously defined humans, too, as "zoon politikon," meaning we are social animals. But our humanity involves more than just living in communities, or forming social arrangements, or practicing the division of labor. We are, fundamentally and inescapably, relational beings.

Across time and culture, societies have imposed penalties and chastisement in the cruel recognition of this fact. Many ancients considered exile from one's community a more grievous penalty than death. Religious groups have practiced excommunication and shunning as the ultimate sanction, and preachers project outer darkness, or isolation from God and loved ones, as a burning beyond hell. In a penal context, many consider solitary confinement a form of psychological torture; in prolonged cases, it can lead to complete mental collapse. The most terrifying specter that haunts the modern psyche is not death or disease or nuclear annihilation. It is loneliness.

We pass through birth and death as individuals. But the years in between are filled with the unceasing search for community, for companionship, for intimacy. There is no self-evident reason why this should be so, and why an existence alone should be fodder not just for melancholy musings, but for nightmares and madness. The myth of Aristophanes, of primeval two-headed quadrupeds that challenged the gods and were sundered in twain as punishment, was simply the projection of a universal suspicion: that we now exist as incomplete beings.

When C. S. Lewis wrote on the four loves, he did not include love of Sicilian pizza or of Turkish baths. He understood that love is most essentially a term that addresses the complex forms of connection we make to other beings, and that those connections are so various and layered that the Greeks needed at least four words to capture what we reduce to one amorphous catchall. (No English word has been more debased than *love*, which we simultaneously employ to describe God's sacrifice of His Son and our feelings about a hot-dog smothered in relish.) Affection, friendship, romance, and charity (*storge*, *philia*, *eros*, and *agape*) dominate our social existence, revealing our lives to be an ongoing, comprehensive effort to find and secure relationships and connections on every conceivable level.

Relationships are the core of our existence because they are the core of God's, and we are in His image. God's nature and life are the simple extension of that which is most elemental, and most worthwhile, about our life here on earth. However rapturous or imperfect, fulsome or shattered, our knowledge of love has been, we sense it is the very basis and purpose of our existence. It is a belonging that we crave because it is one we have always known.

Embracing the ancient connection that binds mortals to God restores to us a glorious beginning and portends a glorious future. It affirms that we are of divine lineage, with a home in the heavens just as the child of royal parents sent in quest of the pearl, with every hope of returning there. This sense of identity makes our search for the divine nature an act of filial love and emulation. And this knowledge gives us, too, a particularly potent reason for the yearning that Sarah Edwards felt to, "with the confidence of a child, and without the least misgiving of heart, call God my Father." It means that "nothing is going to startle us more when we pass through the veil to the other side than to realize how well we know our Father and how familiar His face is to us."

And just as the young man in the Hymn of the Pearl returned to royal parents, so did Eliza R. Snow, an early Mormon poet, capture the sense of a heavenly homecoming that involves a Father *and* a divine Mother.

I had learned to call thee Father,
Thru thy Spirit from on high,
But, until the key of knowledge
Was restored, I knew not why.
In the heav'ns are parents single?
No, the thought makes reason stare!
Truth is reason; truth eternal
Tells me I've a mother there.

A great deal is at stake in the decision to consider ourselves as pre-existing the material universe, as being co-eternal with God. The more common conception that God created the universe and everything (and everyone) in it, called creation ex nihilo, "represented a fundamental change in the Christian understanding of the world," according to Karen Armstrong. It "tore the universe [and us] away from God," making the created order into "an entirely different nature than the substance of the living God."

Making God the source of all that exists, rather than the greatest and best and wisest Being in the universe, destroyed the soul's inherent kinship with the Divine, and introduced the "infinite qualitative difference," the sense of God as "wholly other," that has been common ever since. The God who walked and talked in the Garden with Eve and Adam became with time the God of the theologian Thomas Aquinas, and of the philosopher Simone Weil. "We can know *that* God is and what God is *not* but not *what God is*," said the first. "There is nothing that resembles what she can conceive of when she says the word God," wrote the second.

In some cases, belief in our premortal existence was abandoned precisely because it implied a connection to the divine that was thought to be blasphemous, to span a divide thought to be unbridgeable. The church father Tertullian explicitly rejected preexistence in just such terms. He thought attributing an eternal past to the spirit "put it on a par with God." Making the soul "*unborn*" suggested to his mind perfect divinity, "which properly belonged only to God." A century later, the church father Arnobius agreed that only those with "an extravagant opinion of themselves" believed that souls were not created at birth, but were literally "descended from that parent and sire, divine."

Extravagant or not, the emphasis on a heaven that recovers and extends relationships forged in this life and before, gives meaning and focus to our life in the here and now. Our growth into godliness is a process directed and enabled by God, in accord with an inherent capacity. It is in the continuity of our lives now with our lives hereafter that we find rescue from the dangerous heaven of fairy tales. We say rescue, because a recurrent temptation in Christian history has been to imagine a heaven that is an escape from the hard slog of life, a sudden liberation from life's disappointments, shattered dreams, and wounded relationships.

Nietzsche was right when he said Christians had a tendency to turn away from this life in contempt, to dream of other-worldly delights rather than resolve this-worldly problems. We humans have a lamentable tendency to spend more time theorizing the reasons behind human suffering, than working to alleviate human suffering, and in imagining a heaven above, than creating a heaven in our homes and communities.

"A right faith is an excellent and valuable thing," wrote the early American preacher Jonathan Mayhew, "but it is advantageous no further than it . . . leads us to live an holy and godly life." And that means a life that earnestly engages, rather than distracts us from, our ethical obligations to each other. Pure religion, said James, is to "*care* for widows and orphans," not to sermonize about their plight. This is where Enoch's vision is particularly instructive. It makes heaven, and the process of building it, continuous with the best—but also the most taxing—elements of the present. "There was no poor among them," we read of Enoch's Zion, meaning the foundations of heaven are made of the materials we have at hand, which we transform into a realm of beauty.

In the vision of Enoch, God gave the name of Zion to his abode. And Zion, he told Enoch, was where the earthly and the heavenly societies meet, where "we will fall upon their necks, and they shall fall upon our necks." This vision of heaven as the convergence of two societies, an earthly and a heavenly, is a beautiful template for the work we face as humans: fitting ourselves, our families, our communities, to be participants in a celestial society. What this means is that our present relationships are both the laboratory in which we labor to perfect ourselves and the source of that enjoyment that will constitute our true heaven.

What we call the virtues are precisely those attributes of character that best suit us to live harmoniously, even joyfully, in society. Kindness only exists when there is someone to whom we show kindness. Patience is only manifest when another calls it forth. So it is with mercy, generosity, and self-control. What we may have thought was our private pathway to salvation, was intended all along as a collaborative enterprise, though we often miss the point. The confusion is understandable, since our current generation's preference for "spirituality" over "religion" is often a sleight of hand that confuses true discipleship with self-absorption.

The new sensibility began innocently enough with the lyrical expression of William Blake, who suggested that God might be better found in the solitary contemplation of nature than in the crowded pews of churches. He urged readers "to see the world in a grain of sand, and heaven in a wildflower / hold infinity in the palm of your hand, and eternity in an hour." It took a Marxist critic, Terry Eagleton, to point out that the gospel of Matthew teaches us that "Eternity lies not in a grain of sand but in a glass of water. The cosmos revolves on comforting the sick. When you act in this way, you are sharing in the love which built the stars."

Holiness is found in how we treat others, not in how we contemplate the cosmos. As our experiences in marriages, families, and friendship teach us, it takes relationships to provide the friction that wears down our rough edges and sanctifies us. And then, and only then, those relationships become the environment in which those perfected virtues are best enjoyed. We need those virtues not just here, but eternally because "the same sociality that exists here, will exist there, only it will be coupled with celestial glory, which glory we do not now enjoy."

The project of perfection, or purification and sanctification, is in this light not a scheme for personal advancement, but a process of better filling—and rejoicing in—our role in what Paul called the body of Christ, and what others have referred to as the New Jerusalem, the General Assembly and Church of the Firstborn, or, as in the prophecy of Enoch, Zion. Christians have long employed the term that first appeared in scripture as the Jerusalem stronghold captured by David. Church Fathers read Zion to mean "every holy and godly person" who "is lifted above this life"; Augustine saw the related expression, the New Jerusalem, as a metaphor for the universal church to which all righteous saints belonged.

Puritans used Zion to refer to the godly society they hoped to form in the New World, and by the nineteenth century, Methodists and others employed the term to suggest a godly people or project. Scattered visionaries and eccentrics turned their attention to the task of constructing a literal Zion in the shape of a religious Utopia in the American wilderness. John Hartwick, Jemima Wilkinson ("the Publick Universal Friend") and Robert Matthews ("Matthias") all launched such enterprises in upstate New York. And it was from New York that Smith first transformed his repeated admonitions to "bring forth and establish Zion" into a project of literal community-building.

All who have attempted to reenact Enoch's enterprise have found the transition from worldly ways to celestial society a more taxing challenge than anticipated. The hard lesson has been, that "Zion cannot be built up unless it is by the principles of the law of the celestial kingdom." Rome is not the only city that cannot be built in a day.

So the work of Zion-building continues among all those who seek to do the works of Christ. God our Father authored the blueprint of our development and shepherds us along the path. Christ's atonement makes possible the dynamic process of change, the continual redefining of ourselves through ever better choices and decisions. Obedience to His "gentle commands" is our way of displaying trust in His counsel, and faithfulness effects the gradual changes of heart and mind that move us forward.

The lovely paradox of willing compliance with what an ancient prophet called "the great plan of happiness," is that conformity to law breeds both freedom and individualism. We may think a leaping child, in the euphoria of his imagination, enjoys unfettered freedom when he tells us he is going to land on the moon. But the rocket scientist hard at work in the laboratory, enmeshed in formulae and equations she has labored to master, and slaving away in perfect conformity with the laws of physics, is the one with true freedom: for she will land on the moon; the boy will not.

So too does respect for the principles that undergird reality free us to develop as individuals, making us more, not less, dissimilar from the mass. The whole purpose of learning the moral law in its fullness is to give us the knowledge and the agency to function independently, to choose our own destiny, to be "free to act for [ourselves], and not to be acted upon." William Law wrote that "All kinds of holy living and all kinds of virtue lie open to those who are masters of themselves." In that freedom, we escape the conformity born of fear, the manipulations born of weakness, the bondage born of ignorance. Every wrongheaded impulse moves us in the direction of faceless reaction, blind instinct. As with the scientist mentioned above, the fullest expression of agency can only unfold within the context of moral rigor. And that agency, that moral independence, reveals an authentic self.

Paul is often read as finding in Adam and Eve the seeds of an original sin and corruption of human nature. We read him very differently. In his contemplation of the law, he reveals a remarkably generous view of an inherent goodness at our core, however impeded by human weakness. Unfortunately, the relevant text is one of the most crazily confusing passages he wrote: "For I do not do what I want, but I do the very thing I hate. . . . I can will what is right, but I cannot do it. For I do not do the good I want, but the evil I do not want is what I do. Now if I do what I do not want, it is no longer I that do it, but sin that dwells within me."

At some level, Paul recognizes, in spite of our weak actions and poor choices, the true self, or what he calls the real "I," wants the good, even wills the good, but cannot perform it. If we follow the path of sanctification, the true self, the authentic self, the child of royalty sent in quest of the pearl, will be revealed. The poet Derek Wolcott's words might well describe such a moment: "The time will come when, with elation you will greet yourself arriving at your own door, in your own mirror, and will smile at the other's welcome, and say Sit here. Eat. You will love again the stranger who was yourself."

We will have a mirror that reflects and reveals truly, Wolcott says, not the dim mirror Paul so lamented, obscuring as it did our own reflection. The poet Gerard Manley Hopkins imagined the moment with rather more drama:

> *A heart's-clarion! Away grief's gasping, ' joyless days, dejection.*
> *Across my foundering deck shone*
> *A beacon, an eternal beam. ' Flesh fade, and mortal trash*
> *Fall to the residuary worm; ' world's wildfire, leave but ash:*
> *In a flash, at a trumpet crash,*
> *I am all at once what Christ is, ' since He was what I am, and*
> *This Jack, joke, poor potsherd, ' patch, matchwood, immortal diamond,*
> *Is immortal diamond.*

The moment will be one of recognition, not miraculous transformation. Salvation is a process, not an event. Joseph Addison felt there could be no

> more pleasing and triumphant Consideration in Religion than this of the perpetual Progress which the Soul makes towards the Perfection of its Nature, without ever arriving at a Period in it. To look upon the Soul as going from Strength to Strength, to consider that she is to shine for ever with new Accessions of Glory, and brighten to all Eternity; that she will be still adding Virtue to Virtue, and Knowledge to Knowledge; carries in it something wonderfully agreeable to that Ambition which is natural to the Mind of Man. . . . We know not yet what we shall be.

If in some distant day we discover we have become participants in the Divine Nature, we will only have fulfilled the purposes God set in motion aeons ago when he called us into relationship with Him. As the embodiment of the most perfect love the universe has known, Christ is the model to which we aspire. C. S. Lewis did not think Hopkins's vision unrealistic or inappropriate. As he wrote, "The Church exists for nothing else but to draw men into Christ, to make them little Christs. If they are not doing that, all the cathedrals, clergy, missions, sermons, even the Bible itself, are simply a waste of time. God became Man for no other purpose. It is even doubtful . . . whether the whole universe was created for any other purpose."

When we find we have attained our authentic stature, and only in such authenticity, will we be free to engage in relationships with authentic others. As we engage in those relationships, we find once again that the perfect community of love enhances, rather than diminishes, our differences. "Our ultimate felicity," writes the poet Coventry Patmore, "will consist . . . of innumerable unique . . . individualities, . . . each one shining with its proper lustre, which shall be as unlike any other lustre as that of a sapphire is from that of a ruby or an emerald." This is fortunate, since love is what occurs in the face of difference, not sameness. In God's garden, we will continue to blossom differently. And in that difference, we find a chemistry and a harmony, a spark across the gap, that consumes us all.

What we are most certain of, is that "Our natural affections . . . are the cement of all virtuous and heavenly society." Ultimately, we understand God's nature, and human salvation, to be the simple amplification of that which is most elemental, and most worthwhile, about our life here on earth. The divine nature of man, and the divine nature of God, are shown to be the same—they are rooted in the will to love, at the price of pain, but in the certainty of joy. Heaven holds out the promise of a belonging that is destined to extend and surpass any that we have ever known in this wounded world.

So we learn, and we love. What we have learned, and how we

have loved, endure. Those are the two constants in our continuing existence. "Whatever principle of intelligence we attain unto in this life, it will rise with us in the resurrection." We are not talking of just the book learning of the academy, though that knowledge has its eternal role as well. Nothing learned is wasted, since God is the Master, not the Magician, of the universe, and we strive to become like Him. That is why, as Pratt's brother Orson taught, "The study of science is the study of something eternal. If we study astronomy, we study the works of God. If we study chemistry, geology, optics, or any other branch of science, every new truth we come to the understanding of is eternal; it is a part of the great system of universal truth. It is truth that exists throughout universal nature; and God is the dispenser of all truth—scientific, religious, and political."

More important, will be how we transform such learning into loving. Moving through what Dickinson called "the fair schoolrooms of the sky," we will grow in our knowledge pertaining to successively higher forms of law—without distinction between the laws of physics and the laws of holiness. And it will be a project that opens to us the vision of Heaven as a new beginning, not a final end, to our eternal education. "This is a wide field for the operation of man that reaches into eternity," said Brigham Young. A modern physicist agrees:

> It is reasonable to anticipate that the life of the world to come will not be focused in a timeless moment of illumination, as some eschatological traditions have suggested (the beatific vision), but it will take the form of an evolving salvific process, involving judgment and purgation and leading to the endless exploration of the inexhaustible riches of the divine nature as they are progressively unveiled. If finite creatures are truly to encounter the infinite reality of the divine, it must surely be through such a "temporal" process of this kind. The finite cannot take in the Infinite at a glance.

We believe in a heaven—and heavenly inhabitants—that are dynamic, not static, in their existence. Nothing in the ever-evolving cosmos God has fashioned, nothing in the relentless self-perfecting processes of species and individuals, nothing in the insatiable longings of the human heart, suggests otherwise. Even so, preachers and poets alike have been much more effective at portraying the torments of the damned than the felicities of the blessed. Dante's visualizations of the citizens of hell are unsurpassed. The lustful are wafted on eternal currents of passion, while the vengeful gnaw on the skulls of those who betrayed them. Heaven, by contrast, he lamely describes as great lights, three circles of three colors, more circles of light, and some rainbows, before lamenting "how my weak words fall short of my conception, which is itself so far from what I saw."

Perhaps we cannot succeed where earth's greatest poets fail. Perhaps we cannot envision the full contours of a heaven the mystics have found beyond human reckoning. But Enoch's vision is a useful corrective to the "blue sky heaven" that would seduce us into seeing less continuity between this world and the next than we have good reason to suspect exists. It is not mere wishful thinking but a response to the evidence God has so freely scattered throughout our universe that leads us to believe in heaven as a process that has long been underway, and will continue into the future.

William Wordsworth wrote an account of his quest one summer, in the company of a school friend, to cross the Alps. With youthful vigor and highest hopes, he throws himself into the adventure.

A march it was of military speed,
And earth did change her images and forms
Before us, fast as clouds are chang'd in Heaven.
Day after day, up early and down late,
From hill to vale we dropped, from vale to hill
Mounted—from province on to province swept,

Keen hunters in a chase of fourteen weeks,
Eager as birds of prey, or as a ship
Upon the stretch, when winds are blowing fair:

They pass in sight of the majestic Mount Blanc. They behold "the wondrous Vale of Chamouny," with its "cataracts and streams of ice," and "five rivers, broad and vast." Day after day, and week upon week, they approach the summit, anticipating the joyful climax of their journey. With the goal in sight, they stop for lunch, then linger as their guide moves on ahead. Resuming their trek, they lose the trail, and wander about for some time before happening across a peasant. Asking directions, their confusion turns to disbelief, then disappointment:

we learned
That to the spot which had perplexed us first
We must descend, and there should find the road,
. . .
And, that our future course, all plain to sight,
Was downwards, with the current of that stream.
Loth to believe what we so grieved to hear,
For still we had hopes that pointed to the clouds,
We questioned him again, and yet again;
But every word that from the peasant's lips
Came in reply, translated by our feelings,
Ended in this,—that we had crossed the Alps.

So anxiously were their hearts set upon the distant goal, so certain were they that the destination would shine forth with conspicuous majesty, that they were oblivious to its attainment.

What if we were to find ourselves laboring under a similar delusion? What if in our anxious hope of heaven, we find we have blindly passed it by, like Wordsworth blazing past the alpine summit? What if the possibilities of Zion were already here, and its scattered elements all about us? A child's embrace, a companion's caress, a friend's laughter are its materials. Our capacity to mourn another's pain, like God's tears for His children; our desire to lift our neighbor from his destitution, like Christ's desire to lift us from our sin and sorrow—these are not to pass away when the elements shall melt with fervent heat. They are the stuff and substance of any Zion we build, any heaven we inherit. God is not radically Other, and neither is His heaven.

EPILOGUE

Help Thou Mine Unbelief

A modern revelation, speaking of spiritual gifts, notes that while to some it is given to know the core truth of Christ and His mission, to others is given the means to persevere in the absence of certainty. The New Testament makes the point that those mortals who operate in the grey area between conviction and incredulity are in a position to choose most meaningfully, and with most meaningful consequences.

Peter's tentative steps across the water capture the rhythm familiar to most seekers. He walks in faith, he stumbles, he sinks, but is embraced by the Christ before the waves swallow him. Many of us will live out our lives in doubt, like the unnamed father in the gospel of Mark. Coming to Jesus, distraught over the pain of his afflicted son, he said simply, "I believe, help my unbelief." Though he walked through mists of doubt, caught between belief and unbelief, he made a choice, and the consequence was the healing of his child. "The highest of all is not to understand the highest but to act upon it," wrote Kierkegaard. Miracles do not depend on flawless faith. They come to those who question as well as to those who know. There is profit to be found, and advantage to be gained, even in the absence of certainty. One of our gifted co-religionists writes:

> If Christ has indeed purchased eternal life for humanity, I for one will awaken to the reality of his gift with an immeasurable gratitude. In the meantime, I make it the center of my Christian worship to anticipate that gratitude when I partake of [communion]. . . . It is not an unworthy way of celebrating the Lord's Last Supper to measure one's successes and failures in keeping the commandments and to renew one's covenants to live righteously. Yet in a sense it seems a pity to take one's immortality for granted, to expect it and count on it. It seems a pity to be so sheltered from the terror of death that one's gratitude for the resurrection is merely dutiful and perfunctory. Perhaps truly there are religious advantages to doubt. Perhaps only a doubter can appreciate the miracle of life without end.

Maybe the distance Levi Peterson detects between himself and his religious community is not so great as he thinks. Perhaps the world cannot be so readily divided into believers and doubters. We may be closer to the truth in recognizing that most individuals are divided in their own souls between belief and doubt, just as the father Mark describes. We certainly do not profess any certain knowledge and confess our kinship with Keats. Like him, we know we are "straining at particles of light in the midst of a great darkness." And yet, what we have presented is a version of life's meaning that makes sense to us. We find it reasonable, and resonant—a song that runs deeper than memory.

Notes

A note on sources. Mormons have four volumes of sacred writings, and we have quoted liberally from all of them. Latter-day Saints use the King James Version (KJV) of the Bible, but in this book we have more frequently used the New Revised Standard Version (NRSV) for its greater clarity (and occasional greater accuracy). Particular usage is noted in each citation below. The Book of Mormon (BM) was published in 1830 by Joseph Smith, as a translation of sacred records pertaining to an ancient American people, ca. 600 B.C.–A.D. 421. The Doctrine and Covenants (D&C) is largely a compilation of Joseph Smith's revelations and writings. The Pearl of Great Price (PGP) contains portions of Smith's personal history, as well as writings associated with Moses and Abraham. Prominent among these is an account of the Old Testament patriarch Enoch. Whereas the book of Genesis gives him passing mention, the Book of Moses expands Enoch's story to two full chapters.

Mormons also believe that whatever God's servants "speak when moved upon by the Holy Ghost shall be scripture" (D&C 68:4). Accepting that more liberal sense of inspired writings, we have culled our sources also from a wider tradition that includes Classical, Jewish, Catholic, and Protestant texts.

Introduction: The Longing Soul

"For He satisfyeth" Psalm 107:9, KJV.

"To see the golden sun" William Hazlitt, "On the Feeling of Immortality in Youth," in *Literary Remains of the Late William Hazlitt* (New York: Saunders and Otley, 1836), 246–47.

"in nearly all" James Fitzjames Stephen, *Liberty, Equality, Fraternity* (New York: Holt & Williams, 1873), 331–33.

"He made the angels" Robert Bolt, *A Man for All Seasons* (Oxford: Heinemann, 1960), 74.

"enticed by the one" 2 Nephi 2:16, BM.

Similar to the poet's image of a church bell Gerard Manley Hopkins, "As Kingfishers Catch Fire," *Poems* (New York: Oxford University Press, 1948), 95.

"That you may become participants" 2 Peter 1:4, NRSV.

joint-heirship Romans 8:17, NRSV.

Chapter One: His Heart Is Set upon Us

"For He has set his heart" Job 7:17, KJV.

belief in God is an option This argument, and description of the modern temper, is most extensively made by Charles Taylor, *The Secular Age* (Cambridge: Harvard University Press, 2007).

"that the universe was" Simon Mitton, *Fred Hoyle: A Life in Science* (Cambridge: Cambridge University Press, 2011), xi.

"if it really is true" Joseph Wood Krutch, *The Great Chain of Life* (Iowa City: University of Iowa Press, 2009), 210–11.

"our surplus intellectual" John Polkinghorne, *Belief in God in an Age of Science* (New Haven: Yale University Press, 1998), 2–3.

"My dog's brain" George Bernard Shaw, *Man and Superman: A Comedy and a Philosophy* (New York: Brentano's, 1922), 133.

The Greek playwright Aristophanes Plato, *Symposium* 192c-d, trans. Alexander Nehamas and Paul Woodruff, in *Plato: Complete Works*, ed. John M. Cooper (Indianapolis: Hackett, 1997), 475.

"When God at first" George Herbert, "The Pulley," *The Poems of George Herbert* (Oxford: Oxford University Press, 1961), 150–51.

"our hearts are restless" Augustine *Confessions* I.i, trans. F. J. Sheed (Indianapolis: Hackett, 1993), 218.

"He satisfyeth" Psalm 107:9, KJV.

"getting hell ready" Augustine *Confessions* xl.xii, trans. F. J. Sheed (Indianapolis: Hackett, 1993), 218.

"at the very outset" Augustine, *On Free Choice of the Will* iii.20, trans. Thomas Williams (Indianapolis: Hackett, 1993), 107–09.

Peter Abelard, . . . Blaise Pascal cited in Edward Beecher, *The Conflict of Ages: or, the Great Debate on the Moral Relations of God and Man* (Boston: Phillips, Sampson & Company, 1853), 110–11.

"It is only to be feared" Martin Luther, *The Bondage of the Will* (Lexington, Kentucky: Feather Trail Press, 2009), 68.

"The wrath of God" Jonathan Edwards, "Sinners in the Hands of an Angry God," *The Works of President Jonathan Edwards: with a Memorial of his Life*, ed. Sereno Edwards Dwight, 10 vols. (New York: Carvill, 1830), 7:169–72.

"that Huck Finn" Mark Twain, *Adventures of Huckleberry Finn* (New York: Webster, 1886), 272.

"What do I care" Fyodor Dostoyevsky, *The Brothers Karamazov*, trans. Constance Garnett (New York: Macmillan, 1922), 258.

the maximum mercy "In his justice and mercy, [God] will give us the maximum reward . . . that he can give, and . . . impose upon us the minimum penalty which it is possible for him to impose." J. Reuben Clark, Jr., *Conference Report of the Church of Jesus Christ of Latter-day Saints* (October 1953), 84.

"is not His as well" Elie Wiesel, *The Trial of God* (New York: Schocken, 2004), 127.

"become like one of us" Genesis 3:22, NRSV.

"My presence shall go" Exodus 33:14–17, KJV.

"an earnest desire" Sereno Edwards Dwight, ed., *The Works of President Edwards; with a memoir of His life. . . .* (New York: Carvill, 1830), 1:172–73.

"The Father, too" *Origen: Homilies 1–14 on Ezekiel* 6:6, trans. Thomas P. Scheck (New York: Newman Press, 2010), 92–93.

"body, parts, and passions" The formula is part of the Westminster Confession of Faith, and has been adopted by many denominations. Philip Schaff, *The Creeds of Christendom: The Evangelical Protestant Creeds* (New York: Harper & Brothers, 1877), 487.

"God, in his graciousness" Dante, *Inferno* II, trans. Allen Mandelbaum (New York: Bantam, 1982, 17.

"Did you think joy" C. S. Lewis, *The Great Divorce: A Dream* (New York: Harper Collins, 1946), 132.

"He that hath wife" Francis Bacon, "Of Marriage and Single Life," *Essays* (London: Humphreys, 1900), 28.

"We are never so defenseless" Sigmund Freud, *Civilization and Its Discontents* (New York: Norton, 1989), 33.

"He was aware" Graham Greene, *The Power and the Glory* (New York: Penguin, 1990), 66.

"Look at the heavens" Job 35:5–7, NRSV.

"What are human beings" Psalm 8:4–5, NRSV.

"What is man" Job 7:17, KJV.

"The God of heaven looked" Moses 7:29–37, PGP.

"Comfort me" Pisqa 29, cited by Michael Fishbane, *The Exegetical Imagination: On Jewish Thought and Theology* (Cambridge: Harvard University Press, 1998), 78; Isaiah 40:1, KJV.

"grieved him to his heart" Genesis 6:6, NRSV.

"make me a sanctuary" Exodus 25:8, NRSV.

"Now when Job's" Job 2:11–13, NRSV.

"Perdition, for the heavens" D&C 76:26.

"glorious, yet contracted" George Herbert, "Christmas," 72.

"In all their affliction" Isaiah 63:9, KJV.

"His bowels" Alma 7:12, BM.

"I SHALL know why" Emily Dickinson, "193," *Complete Poems of Emily Dickinson*, ed. Thomas H. Johnson (Boston: Little, Brown and Co., 1960), 91.

Peter, of course Matthew 26:33.

"I have trodden" Isaiah 63:3, NRSV.

"My God, my God" Mark 15:34, NRSV.

"draw all men" 3 Nephi 27:15, BM.

"The Bible directs man" Dietrich Bonhoeffer to Eberhard Bethge, 16 July 1944. In Larry L. Rasmusssen, *Dietrich Bonhoeffer: Reality and Resistance* (Louisville: Westminster John Knox Press, 2005), 17.

"I am Ruth" Ruth 3:8–11, NRSV.

"Bethlehem and in all the borders" Matthew 2:16, NRSV.

"Here am I" Luke 1:42, NRSV.

"Not sealed, but with open" Herbert, "The Pearl," 80.

"control or dominion" D&C 121:37.

"by long-suffering" D&C 121:41–42.

"without compulsory" D&C 121:46.

"to bring to pass" Moses 1:39, PGP.

"God's power rests" Rachael Givens, "Mormonism and the Dilemma of Tragedy," *Patheos*, http://www.patheos.com/blogs/peculiarpeople/2012/05/mormonism-and-the-dilemma-of-tragedy/

"before the beginning" Proverbs 8:23–31, NRSV.

"when the morning stars" Job 38:7, NRSV.

"He doeth not anything" 2 Nephi 26:24, BM.

"I came that they" John 10:10, NRSV.

"Is it not by his" Robinson Jeffers, "The Excesses of God," in *Selected Poetry of Robinson Jeffers*, ed. Tim Hunt (Stanford: Stanford University Press, 2001), 17.

"to be a bird" N. J. Berrill, quoted in Krutch, *Great Chain*, 224.

"created for beauty" Charles Darwin, *The Origin of Species by Means of Natural Selection* (New York: Penguin, 1985), 227.

"I had brought him lunch" James Redfield, "For Wayne Booth at his Religious Memorial Service in Chicago," *Critical Inquiry* 32.2 (winter 2006): 379–80.

"the beasts of the field" D&C 59:16–20.

Chapter Two: Man Was in the Beginning with God

"He has put eternity" This rendering of Ecclesiastes 3:11 varies widely across biblical translations. This is a modification of Young's Literal Translation (YLT), substituting "eternity" for "world" (*olam*), consistent with Strong's Hebrew Dictionary. All other biblical citations are New Revised Standard Version (NRSV) or King James Version (KJV) as indicated.

"Let me but be taught" Lord Byron, "Cain," I.i, *Byron's Complete Poetical Works*, ed. Paul Elmer More (Boston: Houghton Mifflin, 1905), 628.

"For now we see" 1 Corinthians 13:12, KJV.

"We see in a mirror" 1 Corinthians 13:12, NRSV.

"Do you not think" John Keats to George and Georgiana Keats (14 Feb.–3 May 1819), *The Letters of John Keats* (London: Reeves & Turner, 1895), 304.

"My own experience" C. S. Lewis to Mary Van Deusen, 19 March 1955, in *Collected Letters of C. S. Lewis*, ed. Walter Hooper (New York: HarperCollins, 2007), 3:583. For a detailed discussion of pre-existence, with fuller background on the arguments I paraphrase here, see Givens, *When Souls had Wings* (New York: Oxford, 2010).

"How then do I seek You" Augustine, *Confessions* X.xvii–xxi, 186–89.

Only a reminiscence Clement of Alexandria, *Instructor,* 1.6, in Alexander Roberts and James Donaldson, eds., *The Ante-Nicene Fathers* [hereafter ANF] (Grand Rapids: Eerdmans, 1977), 2:217.

"presence which is not" William Wordsworth, "Ode, Intimations of Immortality," *Poetical Works*, ed. Thomas Hutchinson, Ernest de Selincourt (Oxford: Oxford University Press, 1989), 534–45.

wondered if "we liv'd" Samuel Taylor Coleridge, Poem; Letter to John Thelwall (19 November 1796) in *Collected Letters of Samuel Taylor Coleridge*, 6 vols., ed. E. L. Griggs (Oxford: Clarendon, 1956), 1:260–61.

"groping after" Henry More, "On the Praexistency of the Soul," in *The Complete Poems of Dr. Henry More* (1647; repr. New York: AMS, 1967), 119.

"All unrest" Amos Bronson Alcott, "Orphic Sayings," *Dial* 1.1 (July 1840): 87.

"soul, uneasy and confined" Alexander Pope, *Essay on Man* I.3, 1.97 in *Collected Poems*, ed. Bonamy Dobrée (London: Dent, 1975), 184.

"naked and miserable" Friedrich Schiller, *The Robbers*, I.i. trans. F. J. Lamport, in *The Robbers; Wallenstein* (New York: Penguin, 1979), 33.

"I laid me down" Frances Cornford, "Preexistence," in *Modern British Poetry*, ed. Louis Untermeyer (New York: Harcourt, Brace, 1921), 184–85.

"the mystery of that inextinguishable" Julius Müller, *The Christian Doctrine of Sin*, 2 vols., trans. William Urwick (Edinburgh: Clark, 1868), 2:74.

"books & pictures of old" Letter of William Blake to John Flaxman, 21 September 1800, in Geoffrey Keynes, ed., *The Letters of William Blake* (Cambridge: Harvard University Press, 1968), 41–42.

"everything is arranged" Marcel Proust, *Remembrance of Things Past,* trans. G. K. Scott Moncrieff (New York: Random House, 1927), 2:509–10.

"Seeds of light" Nathanael Culverwell, *An Elegant and Learned Discourse on the Light of Nature* (1652), in E. T. Campagnac, *The Cambridge Platonists* (Oxford: Clarendon Press, 1901), 290.

"church bells beyond the stars" Herbert, "Prayer," 44.

"I . . . have the intuition" John Knox, "Pre-Existence, Survival, and Sufficient Reason," *American Philosophical Quarterly* 32.2 (April 1995): 176n.

"odd privilege of existence" Marilynne Robinson, *Absence of Mind: The Dispelling of Inwardness from the Modern Myth of the Self* (New Haven: Yale UP, 2010), 110.

"old soul" George MacDonald, *A Book of Strife, in the Form of The Diary of an Old Soul* (London: Unwin, 1880).

"We are made of material" Joel R. Primack and Nancy Ellen Abrams, *The View from the Center of the Universe* (New York: Riverhead, 2006), 94.

"in places unimaginably distant" More, *Immortality of the Soul*, in *A Collection of Several Philosophical Writings of Dr. Henry More* (New York: Garland, 1978; reprint of London: James Flesher, 1662), 2:111.

"It certainly seems" Immanuel Kant, *Critique of Pure Reason*, trans. Paul Guyer and Allen W. Wood (Cambridge: Cambridge University Press, 1998), B-807–09, 664.

"Have we existed" Percy B. Shelley, "On a Future State," Ernest Rhys, ed., *Essays and Letters by Percy Bysshe Shelley* (London: Walter Scott, nd), 81–82.

"what is incorruptible" David Hume, "On the Immortality of the Soul," *Of the Standard of Taste and Other Essays* (Indianapolis: Bobbs-Merrill, 1965), 162.

The great Jewish rabbi Menasseh Menassah ben Israel, *De Resurrectione Mortuorum*, cited in Johannes van den Berg, "Menasseh ben Israel, Henry More, and Johannes Hoornbeeck on the Pre-Existence of the Soul," *Religious Currents and Cross-Currents: Essays on Early Modern Protestantism*, eds. Jan de Bruijn, Pieter Holtrop, and Ernestine van der Wall (Leiden: Brill, 1999), 68.

"whether it was reasonable" Arthur Henry King, *The Abundance of the Heart* (Salt Lake City: Bookcraft, 1986), 25.

"For is not our first year" Alfred Lord Tennyson, "The Two Voices," 11. 364–84, in *Poetic and Dramatic Works* (Boston: Houghton Mifflin, 1898), 34.

We may be uneasy Alexander Pope, *Essay on Man* I.3,11. 77–80, 97 in *Collected Poems*, ed. Bonamy Dobrée (London: Dent, 1975), 184.

"We had been inexpressibly" "An Impartial Inquirer After Truth," A

Miscellaneous Metaphysical Essay: or, an Hypothesis Concerning the Formation and Generation of Spiritual and Material Beings . . . (London: A. Millar, 1748), 68.

"My impression is that" By kind permission of Philip L. Barlow, "The Veil," unpublished MS, author's possession.

"could have prevented all sin" J. M. Ellis McTaggart, *Some Dogmas of Religion* (London: Edward Arnold, 1906), 165.

"Christ never was" William Law, *The Spirit of Love* (London: G. Robinson and J. Roberts, 1766), 14.

And that freedom is simply As his translator states, Sartre "rejects the notion that God actually exists because . . . it is, at least he believes, inevitably accompanied by a belief in absolutes and a theory of human nature which would determine our destiny." Jean-Paul Sartre, *Being and Nothingness*, trans. Hazel E. Barnes (New York: Citadel, 1956), xxxiv.

"However far back we go" John Wisdom, *Problems of Mind and Matter* (Cambridge: Cambridge University Press, 1963), 130.

"in a sphere beyond the range" Julius Müller, *The Christian Doctrine of Sin*, 2 vols., trans. William Urwick (Edinburgh: Clark, 1868), 2:72–73.

she found the idea Helen M. Smith, "Pre-Existence and Free Will," *Analysis* 3.3 (January 1936), 41.

"however many readers" M. F. Burnyeat, "Other Lives," *London Review of Books* 29.4 (22 February 2007).

"All Intellectual Spirits" Franciscus Palaeopolitanus [Henry More], *Divine Dialogues, containing sundry Disquisitions and Instructions concerning the Attributes of God and his Providence in the World*, 2 vols. (London: James Flesher, 1668), 2:491.

"Now the Lord had shown" Abraham 3:22–26, PGP.

"Man was also" D&C 93:29.

"God, angels and men" Parley P. Pratt, *Key to the Science of Theology* (Liverpool: F. D. Richards, 1855), 33.

"We love Him" 1 John 4:19, NRSV.

"agrees to form them tabernacles" McIntire Minute Book, 28 March 1841, in Andrew F. Ehat and Lyndon W. Cook, eds., *The Words of Joseph Smith: The Contemporary Accounts of the Nauvoo Discourses of the Prophet Joseph Smith* (Orem, Utah: Grandin, 1994), 68.

Chapter Three: We Are That We Might Have Joy

"Sin is behovely" Julian of Norwich, *Sixteen Revelations of Divine Love Shewed to Mother Juliana of Norwich* (London: Paul, Trench, Trübner, 1902), 68.

"The angel hosts" Robert Frost, "Trial by Existence," first published in *A Boy's Will* (New York: Henry Holt, 1913).

"I was unborn" Lord Byron, "Cain," I.i, *Byron*, ed. Jerome J. McGann (Oxford: Oxford University Press, 1986), 885.

the tree *was* Genesis 3:6.

He notes they have Genesis 3:17, KJV, YLT.

as we see in the vision Revelation 22:2.

"Thou mayest choose" Moses 2:21, PGP.

"Adam fell that men" 2 Nephi 2:25, BM.

In the first Christian centuries The Jewish philosopher Philo, the first Christian theologian Origen of Alexandria, and many subsequent writers adopted this interpretation. See *When Souls had Wings*, 184.

The medieval mystic Julian Julian of Norwich, *Showings*, ed. Denise N. Baker (New York: Norton, 2005), XIV.51.

In the Jewish tradition *When Souls had Wings*, 130.

"The purpose of the human soul" Moses de León, *Sefer ha-Mishqal*, ed. Jochanan H. A. Wijnhoven (Ph.D. dissertation, Brandeis University, 1964), 46–47. Cited in Daniel C. Matt, *The Essential Kabbalah: The Heart of Jewish Mysticism* (San Francisco: HarperSanFrancisco, 1995), 148.

"call a life worse" Plato, *Republic* X 617e, trans. G. M. A. Grube, rev. C. D. C. Reeve, in Plato, 1221.

Darwin speculates Darwin, *Origin of Species*, 229–30.

"without contraries, is no progression." William Blake, *The Marriage of Heaven and Hell* (New York: Oxford University Press, 1975), xvi.

"And in that day Adam" Moses 5:10–11, PGP.

"The point where Paul's" Krister Stendahl, *Paul among Jews and Gentiles* (Philadelphia: Fortress Press, 1979), 40–41, 85.

No wonder Harriet Beecher Stowe's Edward Beecher, *The Conflict of Ages: or, the Great Debate on the Moral Relations of God and Man* (Boston: Phillips, Sampson & Company, 1853), 221–23, 552.

"I died the day" Joseph Chaikin and Sam Shepard, *The War in Heaven: Angel's Monologue*, in Sam Shepard, *A Lie of the Mind: A Play in Three Acts; The*

War in Heaven: Angel's Monologue (New York: New American Library, 1987), 137–38.

"Two souls, alas" Johann Wolfgang von Goethe, *Faust,* I11. 1112–1117. In the translation of Walter Arndt (New York: Norton, 1976), 27.

"there is one thing in our soul" Immanuel Kant, *Religion within the Limits of Reason,* trans. Theodore M. Greene (Chicago: Open Court, 1934), 44–45.

"Long time before I," "How like an angel," "But that which most" Thomas Traherne, "The Salutation," "Wonder," "Innocence," in *Selected Writings of Thomas Traherne*, ed. Dick Davis (Manchester: Fyfield, 1980), 19–20, 24–26.

"Why came ye" Parley P. Pratt, *Autobiography of Parley Parker Pratt,* eds. Scot Facer Proctor and Maurine Jensen Proctor (Salt Lake City, Utah: Deseret Book, 2000), 443.

But the body is not Nathaniel Givens finds rich meaning in the etymology of "self-discipline," which in some languages translates as "self-rule" in the sense of domain over a physical kingdom. Unpublished MS, private possession.

"inseparably connected, receive" D&C 93:33.

"Perhaps He goes to sleep" Gregory Nazianzen, "Oration 37," trans. Charles Gordon Browne and James Edward Swallow, *Nicene and Post-Nicene Fathers*, eds. Philip Schaff and Henry Wace (Peabody, Massachusetts: Hendrickson, 1994), 338.

"the world is charged," "Glory be to God" Gerard Manley Hopkins, "God's Grandeur," "Pied Beauty," in *Poems*, 70, 74.

"There is no enjoyment" *Journal of Discourses*, 26 vols., reported by G. D. Watt et al. (Liverpool: F. D. & S. W. Richards et al., 1851–1886; reprint, Salt Lake City: n.p., 1974), 8:128–29.

"The secret of happiness" Bertrand Russell, *The Conquest of Happiness* (New York: Norton, 1996), 125.

"object and design" The expression comes from an unauthenticated letter attributed to Joseph Smith. *History of The Church of Jesus Christ of Latter-day Saints* (Salt Lake City: Deseret Book, 1973), 5:134.

"the great principle of happiness" Smith, *Words*, 60.

"To that dream-like" Jared Curtis, ed., *The Fenwick Notes of William Wordsworth* (London: Bristol Classical Press, 1993), 61–62.

"praise a fugitive" John Milton, *Areopagitica* (London: Longmans, Green: 1873), 33.

"the nearer man approaches" *Evening and Morning Star* 2.17 (February 1834): 135–36.

"natural man" 1 Corinthians 2:14, KJV; "human wisdom" 1 Corinthians 2:13, 12, NRSV.

"divine origin, acts" Immanuel Kant, *Religion within the Limits of Reason*, trans. Theodore M. Greene (Chicago: Open Court, 1934), 44–45.

"When I was a little child" The Song of the Pearl, trans. Han J. W. Drijvers, Robert M. Grant, Bentley Layton, and Willis Barnstone. In Willis Barnstone and Marvin Meyer, *The Gnostic Bible* (Boston: Shambhala, 2003), 388–94.

"are put on earth a little space" William Blake, "The Little Black Boy," *Songs of Innocence and Experience* (Princeton: Princeton University Press, 1998), 2:42.

"the gospel . . . causes" Brigham Young, *Journal of Discourses*, 3:47.

"feast upon [Christ's] love" Jacob 3:2, BM.

"Love bade me welcome" Herbert, "Love (III)," 180.

"that a grateful mind" John Milton, *Paradise Lost* IV.55–57 (Paris: Thunot, 1850), 105.

According to the Talmud Terryl Givens, *When Souls Had Wings: Premortal Life in Western Thought* (New York: Oxford, 2010), 142–43.

"past the perill of the way" Henry More, "On the Praexistency of the Soul," in *The Complete Poems of Dr. Henry More* (1647; repr. New York: AMS, 1967), xxxix.

Chapter Four: None of Them Is Lost

"the Father's will" John 6:39, KJV

"the gate is narrow" Matthew 7:14, NRSV.

"the greater number of Christian" "The Little Number of Those Who Are Saved," St. Leonard of Port Maurice, http://cathom.blogspot.com/2008/09/little-number-of-those-who-are-saved.html

"blasphemy contained" John Wesley, *Sermons on Several Occasions* (New York: J. and J. Harper, 1827), 2:123, 116.

"God's grace is free" George Whitefield, *Works* (London: Edward and Charles Killy, 1771), 55–58.

"If you have sinned" Job 35:6, NRSV.

"Ye have abandoned me" Judges 10:16, NRSV.

"the better angels" Abraham Lincoln's first inaugural address, March 4, 1861.

"What can we do" Corrie ten Boom, *The Hiding Place* (New York: Bantam, 1971), 209–10.

"How if I take it?" *Lawrence of Arabia*, dir. David Lean, Columbia Pictures, 1962.

"I weigh not what ye do" Percy Bysshe Shelley, *Prometheus Unbound* (London: Dent, 1898), 25–6.

"they are eager" Dante, *Inferno* III:121, trans. Allen Mandelbaum (New York: Bantam, 2004), 27.

"contrary to the nature of God" Alma 41:11, BM.

"contrary to the nature of that righteousness" Helaman 13:38, BM.

"all your heart" Matthew 22:37, NRSV.

"I thought, if sin" Julian of Norwich, *Showings*, XII.27.

"Every sin will have" Anne Conway, *The Principles of the Most Ancient and Modern Philosophy concerning God, Christ and the Creatures* VI, ed. and trans. Allison P. Coudert and Taylor Corse (Cambridge: Cambridge University Press, 1996), VII, 42.

"Let me wring your heart" William Shakespeare, *Hamlet*, III.iv (Leipzig: Tauchnitz, 1868), 71.

"As long as I can conceive" George Bernard Shaw, *Man and Superman: A Comedy and a Philosophy* (New York: Brentano's, 1922), 129.

"the recollection of what is better" Clement of Alexandria, *Instructor*, 2:217.

"of doing as we like" John Stuart Mill, *On Liberty*, 2d edition (Boston: Ticknor and Fields, 1863), 28.

"men are instructed" 2 Nephi 2:5, BM.

"We may think our tribute" The words are cited secondhand in numerous sources, including *Singing the Living Tradition* (Boston: Unitarian Universalist Association, 1993), 561.

"incapable of thinking otherwise" William Law, *A Serious Call to a Devout and Holy Life; The Spirit of Love* (New York: Paulist Press, 1978), 394.

"shall return again to their" D&C 88:32.

"That which is governed" D&C 88:34–35.

"we have no claim" Smith, *Words*, 205.

"that the tenderer parts" William James, *Pluralistic Universe* (Lincoln: University of Nebraska Press, 1996), 307.

"to bind up the brokenhearted" Isaiah 61:1–3, KJV.

"I lay down my life" John 10:15; 12:32, NRSV.

"poured out for many" Matthew 26:28, NRSV.

"an angel from heaven" Luke 22:43–44, NRSV. Scholars dispute the authenticity of this biblical passage; LDS scripture affirms that on this occasion, the weight of the atonement caused Christ "to bleed from every pore" (D&C 19:18).

"Ev'n God himself" George Herbert, "The Bunch of Grapes," 118–19.

"by his bruises" Isaiah 53:5, NRSV.

"suffered these things" D&C 19:16.

"How uncomfortable a thought" John Wesley, *Sermons on Several Occasions* (New York: J. and J. Harper, 1827), 2:119.

"serious theological and liturgical" "The Hope of Salvation for Infants Who Die Without Being Baptized," International Theological Commission, http://www.vatican.va/roman_curia/congregations/cfaith/cti_documents/rc_con_cfaith_doc_20070419_un-baptised-infants_en.html

"God, whose nature is Love" Profession of Faith of the General Convention of Universalists, 1803, Winchester, New Hampshire, Article II, citing Rev. A. B. Grosh, "Universalists" and I. Daniel Rupp, *An Original History of the Religious Denominations* (Philadelphia, 1844), 727.

"unless He intended to make" Charles Chauncy, *The Mystery Hid from Ages and Generations Made Manifest . . . , or, the Salvation of All Men* (London: 1784; repr. Bedford, Massachusetts: Applewood, 2009), preface.

"'Tis true," Chauncy conceded Chauncy, 192.

"weakens and undermines" *New York Times*, 26 July 1863. Reprinted from the *Boston Journal*, 23 July 1863. http://www.nytimes.com/1863/07/26/news/the-trial-of-rev-charles-beecher-he-is-convicted-of-heresy-result.html?pagewanted=all

"not only live, move, and think" Parley P. Pratt, sermon, 7 April 1853, papers of George D. Watt, Latter-day Saint Church History Library.

"the gospel was preached also" 1 Peter 4:6, NRSV.

"accidental truths of history" Gotthold Lessing, "On the Proof the Spirit and of Power," Lessing's Theological Writings, trans. Henry Chadwick (Stanford: Stanford University Press, 1957), 53.

"The work of love" Søren Kierkegaard, *Works of Love: Some Christian Reflections* (New York: HarperCollins, 1964), 320.

Krister Stendahl expressed Remarks reported by Prof. Daniel Peterson, http://

www.fairlds.org/authors/johnson-cooper/breaking-the-rules-critics-of-the-lds-faith. Stendahl in fact wrote the article on Baptism for the Dead for the *Encyclopedia of Mormonism* (New York: Macmillan, 1992), 1:97.

"This is the father's will" John 6:39–40, NRSV.

Samuel was called 1 Samuel 3.

It took a bright light Acts 9.

as a hen its chicks Matthew 23:37.

"His hand is stretched out" Isaiah 10:4, KJV. Many commentators read the expression to reflect continuing anger. We read it, as does the 1568 Bishop's Bible, as signaling a continuing disposition to forgive: "the wrath of the Lord [does not] cease, *but yet* is his hand stretched out still." That reading also comports with Jesus' reference to his repeated efforts to gather in his children like a hen its chicks, in spite of their persistent wickedness.

"the only ones" D&C 76:39, 44.

"turn the hearts of parents" Malachi 4:6, NRSV.

"God will force" "Know This, That Every Soul is Free," in *Hymns of The Church of Jesus Christ of Latter-day Saints* (Salt Lake City: The Church of Jesus Christ of Latter-day Saints, 1985), no. 240.

"the children . . . who had to die" Louis Ginzberg, *Legends of the Bible* (New York: Simon and Schuster, 1956), 601.

preached to the spirits 1 Peter 3–4.

"neither death, nor life" Romans 8:38–39, NRSV.

"God, lover of souls" Gerard Manley Hopkins, "In the Valley of the Elwy," *Poems* (New York: Oxford University Press, 1948), 76.

"God hath made a provision" Joseph Smith, *Words*, 360.

Chapter Five: Participants in the Divine Nature

God "found Himself" Joseph Smith, quoted in Stan Larson, "The King Follett Discourse: a Newly Amalgamated Text," *BYU Studies* 18.2 (winter 1978): 204.

"raise [his] throne" Isaiah 14:13, NRSV.

"build a tower" Genesis 11:4, NRSV.

"infinite qualitative difference" Søren Kierkegaard, *Sickness unto Death* (Radford, Virginia :Wilder, 2008), 106.

"the deepest and most fundamental" Rudolf Otto, *The Idea of the Holy*, 2d ed., trans. J. W. Harvey (London: Oxford University Press, 1950), 12–13, 28, 146.

"incredible folly" Augustine, *Confessions* IV.xv, 63.

"the most high" Job 37:16, NRSV.

"highly exalted" Philippians 2:9, KJV.

to be perfect Matthew 5:48.

"Be imitators of God" Ephesians 5:1, NRSV.

"Beloved, we are God's" 1 John 3:2, NRSV.

"becoming like god" Plato, *Theaetetus* 176a, trans. M. J. Levett, rev. Myles F. Burnyeat, in *Plato: Complete Works*, ed. John M. Cooper (Indianapolis: Hackett, 1997), 195.

"He who framed" Plato, *Timaeus* 29e, trans. Donald J. Zeyl in *Plato: Complete Works*, ed. John M. Cooper (Indianapolis: Hackett, 1997), 1236.

"It must be a project" Joseph Addison, "Immateriality of the Soul," *The Spectator* 111 (7 July 1710), 145.

"precious and very great" 2 Peter 1:4, NRSV.

"And it came to pass that the Lord" Moses 7:41–64, PGP.

"was yet a great way" Luke 15:20, KJV.

"the earthly is the image" Smith, *Words*, 232; D&C 128:13.

"that which is temporal" Joseph Smith quotes Paul to this effect, in D&C 127:13; D&C 77:2.

"bound in heaven" Matthew 16:19, NRSV.

"Divine families encircled" Truman G. Madsen, "Are Christians Mormon?" *BYU Studies* 15.1 (autumn 1974): 89.

"The glory that you have given" John 17:22, NRSV.

"And the Lord called his people" Moses 7:18, PGP.

"our natural affections" An appeal to the inhabitants of the state of New York, letter to Queen Victoria, (reprinted from the tenth European edition,) the fountain of knowledge; immortality of the body, and intelligence and affection (Nauvoo, Illinois: John Taylor, 1844), 37–38.

"zoon politikon" Aristotle, *The Politics*, Book 1, Ch. 2.

"nothing is going to startle" Ezra Taft Benson, paraphrasing Brigham Young, "Jesus Christ—Gifts and Expectations," in *Speeches of the Year, 1974* (Provo: Brigham Young University Press, 1975), 313.

"I had learned to" Eliza R. Snow, "Invocation," *Poems, Religious, Historical, and Political* (Liverpool: F. D. Richards, 1856), 2.

"represented a fundamental" Karen Armstrong, *The Case for God* (New York: Anchor, 2010), 105.

"We can know *that* God is," "There is nothing" Aquinas and Weil are paraphrased by Elizabeth A. Johnson, *She Who Is: The Mystery of God in Feminist Theological Discourse* (New York: Crossroad, 1992), 7.

"put it on a par" Tertullian, *Treatise on the Soul* XXIV (ANF 3:203).

"an extravagant opinion" Arnobius, *Against the Heathen* II.15, in Alexander Roberts and James Donaldson, eds., *The Ante-Nicene Fathers* (Grand Rapids: Eerdmans, 1977), 6:440, 420.

"A right faith" Jonathan Mayhew, *Seven Sermons* (Boston: Rogers and Fowle, 1749), 145.

Pure religion James 1:27, NRSV.

"There was no poor" Moses 7:18, PGP.

"To see the world" William Blake, "Augeries of Innocence," in John Sampson, ed., *Poetical Works* (Oxford: Clarendon Press, 1905), 288.

"Eternity lies not" Terry Eagleton, *A Very Short Introduction to the Meaning of Life* (New York: Oxford University Press, 2008), 95.

"the same sociality" D&C 131.

"every holy and godly" Chrysostom, *Proof of the Gospel* 6.24, in Erik M. Heen and Philip D. W. Krey, eds., *Ancient Commentary on Scripture* vol. 10, *Hebrews* (Downers Grove, Illinois: InterVarsity Press, 2005), 223.

"Zion cannot be built" D&C 105:5.

"the great plan of happiness" Alma 42:8, BM.

"free to act" 2 Nephi 2:26, BM.

"All kinds of holy living" William Law, *Serious Call*, 89.

"For I do not do" Romans 7:15–20, NRSV.

"The time will come" Derek Wolcott, "Love After Love," *Collected Poems 1948–1984* (New York: Macmillan, 1986), 328.

"A heart's-clarion!" Gerard Manley Hopkins, "That Nature Is a Heraclitean Fire," in *Poems*, 111–12.

"more pleasing and triumphant" Joseph Addison, "Immateriality of the Soul," *The Spectator* 111 (7 July 1710), 145.

"The Church exists for nothing else" C. S. Lewis, *Mere Christianity* (New York: HarperCollins, 2001), 199.

"Our ultimate felicity" Coventry Kersey Dighton Patmore, *The Rod, the Root, and the Flower* (London: George Bell, 1895), 194–95.

"Our natural affections" Parley P. Pratt, An Appeal to the Inhabitants of the State of New York; Letter to Queen Victoria; The Fountain of Knowledge; Immortality of the Body; and Intelligence and Affection (Nauvoo, Ill.: John Taylor, [1844]), 37.

"Whatever principle of intelligence" D&C 130:19.

"The study of science" Orson Pratt, *Journal of Discourses*, 7:157.

"This is a wide field" Young, *Journal of Discourses*, 9:242.

"It is reasonable" John C. Polkinghorne, *Theology in the Context of Science* (New Haven: Yale University Press, 2009), 156.

"how my weak words" Dante, *Paradise* XXXIII.121, in *Portable Dante*, trans. and ed. Mark Musa (New York: Penguin, 1995), 584.

"A march it was" Wordsworth, *The Prelude* VI.491–99; 579–91, *Poetical Works*, 534–45.

Epilogue: Help Thou Mine Unbelief

Speaking of spiritual gifts "To some it is given by the Holy Ghost to know that Jesus Christ is the Son of God, and that he was crucified for the sins of the world. To others it is given to believe on their words, that they also might have eternal life if they continue faithful," D&C 46:13–14.

"I believe, help" Mark 9:24, NRSV.

"The highest of all" Robert Bretall, *A Kierkegaard Anthology* (New York: Modern Library, 1946), 281.

"If Christ has indeed" Levi S. Peterson, "A Christian by Yearning," *The Wilderness of Faith* (Salt Lake City: Signature, 1991), 125, 134.

"straining at particles" John Keats to George and Georgiana Keats (14 Feb.–3 May 1819), *The Letters of John Keats* (London: Reeves & Turner, 1895), 304.

Index

INDEX